# SURVIVING DEATH

## Eternal Consciousness and the Self-Perpetuating Universe

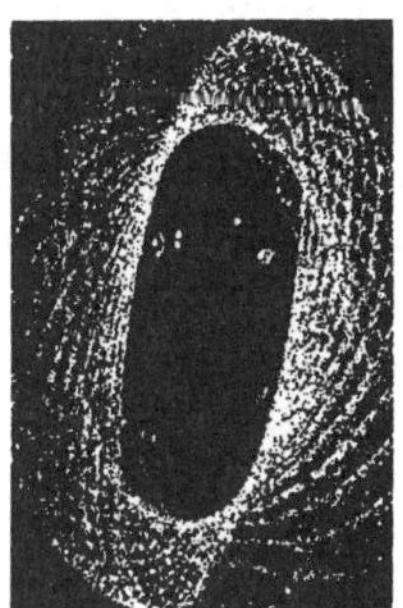

J. Robert Adams, M. Sc., Ph.D., M.D.

To order, tel.
1-800-898-7886

Sterling House Publisher
Pittsburgh, PA

**Sterling House Trade Paperback**

ISBN 1-156315-082-4



First Printing—1998

Request for information should be addressed to:

Sterling House Publisher
The Sterling Building
440 Friday Road
Department T-101
Pittsburgh, PA 15209

Cover design & Typesetting: Drawing Board Studios



For information about Surviving Death and other related topics of interest you can contact the author at Surviving@Polyinter.com

Printed in the United States of America

# TABLE OF CONTENTS

# DEDICATION

To Alexandra


# ACKNOWLEDGEMENTS

Thanks to Celia Milne who first accepted for publication the article on which this book is based; to Douglas Storey for his literary advice to a novice; to Sandy Adams for indispensable assistance at every turn; to Aaron Remer for type scanning; and to Joe Graham for helpful criticisms regarding sequence. Acknowledgement is also made to those scientists and authors (see bibliography) whose work provides a foundation for this book.

# FOREWORD

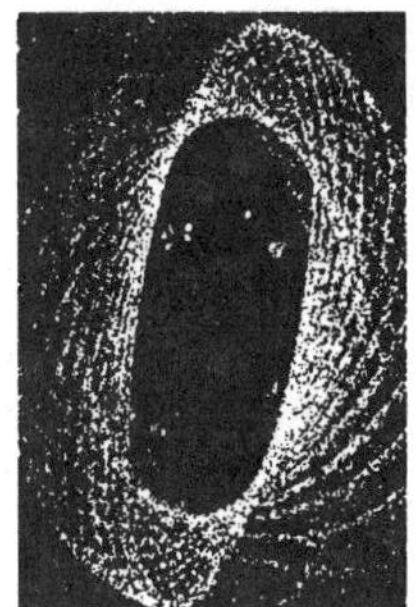

Dr. Adams has asked me to write a foreword to this book. I have never written a foreword before, and Dr. Adams has not even suggested what he would want this foreword to do. So, reader-about-to-be, should I write to you in the role of guide? Advertiser? Critic? Interpreter? Should this foreword forewarn you? Forearm you?

No, I foreswear each and all of these worthy tasks. They would take too many words. They are better left to reviewers. And, most important of all, any of these roles would potentially insert me, another reader and a likely distorting filter, between you and this author.

I can do a little better, I believe, than write to forsake you to your own wits. I've read this book twice, and some sections of it several times, so I think I'm not exceeding my bounds when I tell you that you'll need all your wits about you if you choose to follow Dr. Adams. He starts with a question that people all over the world have asked and faced century after century, since the dawn of human thought: the question of existence after death. He faces this question not with a dogmatic affirmation or denial nor with some fervently professed belief. He has rather chosen to track this centuries-old question with an hypothesis that memory is saved, and in that preservation existence perdures.

This book is quite like the author reaching back, taking the reader by the hand, and basically saying: "Come here and look there and don't you see all these clues that maybe this hypothesis is really the way things are?" The here and the there covered by the tracking are some of today's most advanced of the sciences: molecular biology, the neurosciences, quantum physics, cosmology.

That said, I'll now back off just a little from my refusal to do a forewarning. I think your experience may well be like mine. At first I did not want to take the time to read this book, I did not want to grasp the author's outstretched hand. Once I did, I could not leave off the tracking. The question, "Where is he going next?" persisted and pressed me on to follow Dr. Adams right to the end.

And where do you end up with this book? Stimulatingly not, I think, where Dr. Adams in the introduction thinks the tracking is heading. He suggests that this book is on a course towards resolving the paradox that the saved memory hypothesis can be compatible both with contemporary science and long-standing religious doctrines.

That is not where I found myself after following Dr. Adams, and I am thankful to him. I would have been flattened and bored to have found myself in some clear open space emptied of all the tense forces between the different ways of human knowing that have developed over the centuries. These tensions shape the human quest for meaning and understanding in the most complex of ways, somewhat like the forces of gravity give curvature to space. Those curvatures may be relatively gentle as in the region of our solar system, or bafflingly voracious, as in the proximity of a black hole.

So I back off again from my refusal to forewarn. I do not think you can follow Dr. Adams passively, simply nodding approvingly or even in wonder as he links his hypothesis to this or that domain of science. As you grasp his hand to follow on, his foot is arching back to give you a good kick in the backside. The kick, translated, says: "Go on, start thinking for yourself. But don't abandon the question, even if you don't like my hypothesis."

The complexity of this book is its power. The author sets out to resolve, to clear up a paradox, but, in the end, he does something quite different and much more. He reopens minds, perhaps quite closed in this postmodern age, to rethink an ancient and enduring question. So, reader, beware! If you choose to rethink this question, whether you follow Dr. Adams' tracking or whether you veer off on some unforeseen tangent, you will likely contribute to thickening rather than dissolving the author's paradox. The persistence of Dr. Adams' reopened question, and the stubborn tracking of that question in thought, and perhaps in agony, have clearly survived the deaths of billions of human beings. Another clue, perhaps, that Dr. Adams may be on a promising track with his hypothesis?

David J. Roy
Director, Centre for Bioethics
Clinical Research Institute of Montreal

Editor-in-Chief
Journal of Palliative Care

Professor Faculty of Medicine, Universit, de Montr,al

# INTRODUCTION

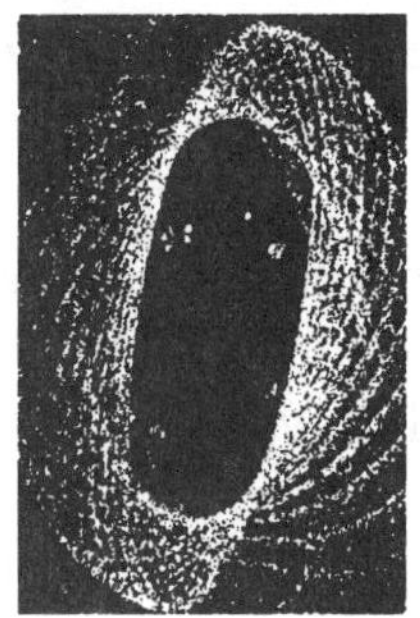

From the moment we are conceived by the union of egg and sperm, the countdown begins toward death. Does consciousness survive death? Life after death is, of course, a contradiction in terms. Death, by definition, is the end of life, so how can we talk about life after death? The Reader, if like most readers, is part realist and part dreamer. The realist part acknowledges that life functions in absolute conformity with the laws of physics and chemistry, and speculation about anything else is nonsense. The dreamer, on the other hand, wants to believe in an imaginary hereafter, a never-never land where his presence would *seem* to violate every known principle of science.

The word 'seem' is italicized, because the violation is only apparent. At least, such is the Hypothesis of this book, which postulates that the Self we know in life survives death without missing a beat and without violating any of Nature's laws.

We can almost hear the skeptic's comment: "Get real, Buster!" We hasten to assure such a person that we don't intend to rally religious or mystical arguments in support of our hypothesis, but rather to extrapolate from the known facts of technology and science. These facts indicate the possibility, without pointing to the probability, that a continuation of subjective consciousness of our Earthly identity survives death.

If, in the pages that follow, we do not always appear to be doggedly sticking to our subject of life after death, it is because 'life' is a difficult and elusive term that needs to be looked at from various points of view. Only then can the prospects for its survival beyond death be credibly analyzed.

Our hypothesis, which we call the Saved Memory Hypothesis, does not appear to the author to contradict any scientific principle, nor to be incompatible with religious doctrine. If this all-inclusive embrace seems strange or at odds with conventional wisdom, we can only suggest that the book will resolve the paradox.

# IDENTITY, DEATH, & EXISTENCE AFTER DEATH

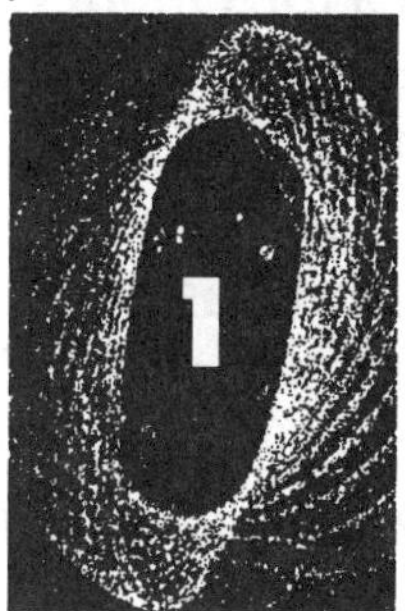


When the Authorities gave us a body, they made it squishy. This is strange, because we don't think of ourselves as squishy. We seem to regard our Self, the 'I' of us, as a dry, pristine entity quite detached from wet, messy things like blood and guts. Yet blood and guts is what we are. The Practical man with the gimlet eye and hard-nosed approach will say: "What you see is what you get, my friend, which is only liquid with a few solids thrown in." "Wrong," corrects the Romantic, "there is more. There is the spirit, the immortal Self, for which the wet body is only a temporary abode, a stopping-off place."

This controversy, and the concept of a dichotomy between body and spirit, is ancient. A person's thoughts appear to him to be ethereal, immortal aspects of his identity that exist in a separate dimension and have little to do with the body which, in its turn, strikes him as a coexisting object vulnerable to all the dangers of a hostile world.

We are not normally bothered by the fact that the Self resides in, and thoughts are dependent upon, a milieu of blood and guts. Not bothered, that is, until an awareness of the extreme vulnerability of the body is forced upon us by some threat which the Self cannot control. Then we are likely to be overcome with panic, since any threat to the body is perceived as a potential annihilation of the Self.

Oddly enough, the human reaction to this situation is frequently to faint. As a first year medical student, I watched a procedure in which an accumulation of fluid called ascites was drained from the belly of a forty eight year old man with cirrhosis of the liver. Unflappable beneath a shock of gray hair, he sat on a high wooden stool with a bright metal pail positioned on the floor in front of him. The fascinated students pressed forward in a ring around the staff doctor as he picked up a sharp stainless steel instrument called a trocar and with it penetrated the abdomen of the patient. All eyes were riveted on the jet of straw-yellow liquid that suddenly spurted out of the man's belly, missed the pail, and splattered onto the floor. The doctor kicked with his foot and the pail clattered noisily into place. This was all too wet and squishy for me. I collapsed in a heap as the patient dryly observed: "A fine doctor he'll make."

Another story about fainting involves Hitler's Gestapo chief Himmler. Five newly minted SS guards, resplendent in tailored gray uniforms and polished black boots, were inspecting a pathetic assembly of concentration camp inmates dressed in putrid rags. Himmler pulled his pistol from its oiled leather holster. He handed the pistol to the nearest guard, pointed his finger at an inmate, and ordered: "Shoot him." The rookie hesitated. Himmler seized the gun, positioned it barely inches from the prisoner' s head, and fired. Pink-gray bits of brain spattered onto the rookie's uniform, and he promptly fainted. Why? The vulnerability of life had been dramatized all too graphically and he could not cope.

But we adapt with frequent exposure to the sight of death. Again using first year medical students as an example, it is not uncommon to see one or two students faint as they initially file into the dissecting laboratory for their first encounter with human cadavers. By the end of the year, their behavior is quite different. Accustomed to the daily routine of dissection, the hardened students seek distraction by propping up their cadaver and placing the morning newspaper in its hands, or tossing bits of tissue at one another. The dried out, worked over remnants of once living flesh cease to remind students of their own personal vulnerability.

These anecdotes underline our sensitivity to the fact that our body is vulnerable to harm and destruction. We are sitting ducks. And since we know that the Self is linked to the body, we feel that our identity could be wiped out at any moment whether by disease, accident, or other cause. Sensing that death could come simply by a capricious roll of the dice, we are inclined to wonder why we are alive in the first plaçe. Is it by chance, or design? If we can be alive one moment and dead the next, has anything important been accomplished by our existence?

The Danish philosopher Kierkegaard must have been reflecting upon this when he wrote:

'Where am I? Who am I? How did I come to be here? What is this thing called the world? ....How did I come into the world? Why was I not consulted? ... And if I am compelled to take part in it, where is the manager? I would like to see him.'

We can reflect similarly about the end of life. Do we survive death? If so, what survives? Where, and why? What happens then? Enigmas of this kind have wrinkled brows down through the ages from primitive to modern people. Only the human being, the present king of the animal world, has the brain power to ask such questions. Throughout most of history, we have sought answers through speculation. Because speculation can not yield definitive data, we finally took a new fork in the road marked Science. Mankind started down this fork about four centuries ago, at first haltingly, then with increasing assurance, and has seldom looked back.

Most of us believe this choice was a good one. If we want to probe mysteries, the only known way that is reliable is the method of controlled observation and deduction; that is, by scientific investigation. This method has yielded extraordinary results over the last few centuries, and it seems we have only made a few scratches on the surface of what is to be known. The mystical and speculative part of our history was useful in smoothing over life's anxieties, but did not provide solid information upon which to build an understanding of our world. A religious person with deep faith will proclaim: "God is in His heaven, and when I die I will join Him there." But the agnostic asks the believer: "Upon what evidence do you base your opinion?" Another believer, the reincarnationist, declares his belief by saying: "My life, everybody' s life, is lived in a consecutive series of bodies which have preceded, and which will succeed, the present one." Again the skeptic inquires: "What is the evidence that leads you to this conclusion?"

Literature exists in vast quantities in our libraries on the subject of religion and various concepts of the supernatural. Yet, the only dependable method we have found to understand the universe is to painstakingly dissect out the pieces one by one and examine them at high magnification under controlled conditions. Since, paradoxically, we form a part of the environment that we are examining, our scrutiny encompasses the study of ourselves. In any such study, the *subjective* awareness that makes up our conscious Self must be correlated with the mechanisms in the brain that are responsible for producing the awareness. Our thoughts depend on these brain mechanisms which involve physical and chemical processes. They cannot be investigated only through introspection, but require *objective* study as well.

Francis Crick believes that the secrets of the complex and fascinating neural mechanisms underlying consciousness can be unraveled in the laboratory. Crick, along with James Watson in 1953, launched modern molecular biology by discovering the structure of DNA, life's template. Dr. Crick is currently investigating the relationship between consciousness and optical imagery. Other investigators of consciousness are building upon the finding of Donald Hebb that nerve pathways are strengthened through use ('use it, or lose it'). Still other researchers have found that nerves grow and new connections form during learning. In short, people in many laboratories are probing the mysteries of memory and consciousness in a new effort to penetrate this previously impervious frontier. This book will look over the shoulders of lab workers dealing with action potentials and chemical fluxes. Also, its focus will be on subjective self awareness which is the *product* of, and must be correlated with, the physical and chemical processes that go on in the brain.

Science is not in any way incompatible with belief in God. Sir Isaac Newton was a strong believer in God, yet he had one of the greatest scientific minds of all time. In other words, whether God exists, and if 'He' is male, female, black, yellow, white, incorporeal, or something in between, is presently a matter of personal judgment and does not encroach on the domain of science. Science is concerned only with understanding information that is gathered directly or indirectly through the five human senses. It does not concern itself with abstract issues that are beyond its competence to verify.

Before the scientific method offered a rational alternative to mysticism, man could hardly be criticized for grasping at straws. His plight might be likened to that of the unfortunate passengers of the Titanic who, on the tragic night of April 14, 1912, found themselves floundering in the cold black waters of the Atlantic with little prospect for survival. We can imagine them desperately clutching — a cushion, a stray piece of debris — any support no matter how flimsy to help them stay afloat. For early man, speculation and mysticism certainly offered support. But that support was frail and provided scant rescue from an ocean of ignorance.

In the twentieth century, the unique human brain is acquiring knowledge at the exponential rate of a rocket lifting off its launch pad. So far, humans have had no influence upon the operation of the universe at large. They have changed their tiny speck of a planet, walked their tiny moon, and sent information probes to the far reaches of their tiny solar system. But these achievements, huge in their own eyes, have not made waves in the universe. This invisibility of human effort may be temporary. It is tempting to predict that our intelligence will ultimately make its presence felt over vast distances and perhaps more seriously alter the destiny of the universe. This depends, of course, upon our continuing existence. Does mankind, in fact, have a future?

Fred Hoyle is a well known British astronomer who feels that intelligent beings, wherever and whenever they exist in the cosmos, blow themselves up soon after they achieve the capacity to do so. The human race, he somberly notes, now has this capacity. Despite Hoyle's despairing philosophy, the accumulation of man's knowledge is accelerating. Barring a Hoyle-like disaster or other unpredictable catastrophe, man's science, if allowed to proceed on track, may ultimately answer our questions about life and death. Obtaining information through ongoing research is time spent more wisely than waiting around for a message from outer space, more productively than pursuing the mystic delusions of ancient man.

This book embarks on a voyage of discovery. The reader is urged to pry into and tease apart ideas that timid souls prefer to leave undisturbed. Ideas concerning life, death, and identity are dealt with without pulling any punches. These form a springboard for the leap to a new hypothesis: creation has ensured the survival of personal identity after death based on memory recapture. This hypothesis does not violate the ideas of God, or Science. It offers the possibility of the 'life' after death that most of us hope for, a post-mortem existence consistent with both religious belief and natural law.

Karl Popper, a strongly opinionated contemporary philosopher, considered that a hypothesis cannot be categorized as science, but only pseudo-science, unless it is testable. The hypothesis presented in this book for survival after death cannot at present be tested. But the disciplines needed to test it—these include neurophysiology, quantum theory, information theory, and artificial intelligence—are advancing by leaps and bounds. The hypothesis may eventually qualify for Popper's precise picture of science. Depending on the outcome of future experimentation, a valid model for survival after death may become apparent. Or, the hypothesis may be junked along with other ideas that have been proved wrong.

Whatever the eventual outcome, the search for answers is both compelling and fascinating.

# A HYPOTHESIS FOR SURVIVAL AFTER DEATH

## "I DON'T WANT TO DIE"

Did you see the old black and white film starring James Cagney in which a murderer (Cagney) is dragged to the electric chair ('Old Sparky' at Sing Sing) screaming at the top of his lungs: "I don't want to die"? It was a scary scene, and a dramatic reminder that evolution has programmed all of us to embrace life, not death.

To fear death is natural and has an evolutionary advantage. If we did not have this fear, our species would never have become established because its members wouldn't reach mating age. The fear of death is fundamental to our survival. But because fear of anything, including death, is unpleasant, some of us try to be ingenious and duck the issue of rotting corpses by pretending we don't die — that 'death' is just a bad joke our bodies must endure before we go on to bigger, better things. We imagine that we are immortal. We believe that somehow, somewhere, there is another life.

Is that the same thing as believing in the tooth fairy?

"No," say the scriptures. "The spirit is, indeed, immortal, and this can be accepted on *faith*." Well, there are of course a large number of doubters, atheists, agnostics, and assorted skeptics who do not have this faith. They cry out: "Rubbish! To see is to believe, and we see nothing that is immortal."

And so the debate goes on.

Does classical science do anything to resolve the controversy? Unfortunately not. Classical science sees our universe as an observable, measurable thing where events unfold according to cause and effect with no room for spirits or spooky places. But this may be changing. Since Bohr's insight in the 1920's into *quantum* energy levels, classical science has begun to modify some of its rigid views. Using the new tool of quantum mechanics, science has in a sense gone full circle. Quantum mechanics suggests that we live, after all, in a somewhat fuzzy, indeterminate universe of effect without apparent cause. As far as science is concerned, the question of 'life' after death remains wide open.

**IS THERE LIFE AFTER DEATH?**

The world that we know is a world where death is final. We die, and the only evidence of our former life is, firstly, a decaying corpse, secondly, the recollections of those that remember us, and thirdly, the changes that we may have made to the world when we were alive. There is no credible sign that the life that was is any more.

But we need to believe. In order to allay our fear of death, we take refuge in speculation. Some of us speculate that the soul leaves the body and survives in an unseen world, distinct and separate from our own, such as the heaven of religious parable. Since this other world is imaginary, it can be whatever we wish it to be. Unlike the world of our senses, there are no constraints to its parameters other than the inventiveness of the human mind that conceives it. The better we make it look, the less are we bothered by the specter of death.

Would it not be reassuring if at least part of our conjecture was rooted in actual observation? Although those of absolute faith may not desire such support, the 'I'm from Missouri' crowd would prefer it. For the latter, the following paragraphs will attempt to show how it is possible to anticipate personal existence after death based on rational extrapolation of what we already know. The faithful, whose beliefs need no bolstering, may nevertheless find our material arguments for personal survival philosophically interesting.

**SAVED MEMORY**

*'If immortality is what you crave, then you are much better off with the conception of yourself as fundamentally defined by information, rather than as a sort of immutable mind pearl, or soul of some sort.'*

(Daniel C. Dennett, author of Consciousness Explained).

When we talk about surviving death, what are we talking about? What could survive?

The thing that interests us is the sense of identity, consciousness, or Self that we consider to be our essence. That is the candidate that most of us would like to nominate for immortality.

Now, this candidate (the Self) depends on memory for its existence. Wipe the memory banks clean, and our sense of Self must be built up again from scratch. Therefore, if an awareness of our earthly identity is to survive death, so must our memory. How might this be possible?

The memory is not a black box like Descartes' pineal gland, localized at one brain spot. Rather, it is a distributed system extending here and there throughout the cerebrum. This does not mean that memory is nebulous and undefined. On the contrary, it has a physical structure consisting of a vast assembly of nerves and their trillions of synaptic connections. This network of nerves and synapses stores information — say the color of your dog's nose — in the sense that the information can be presented *again* to the consciousness by the firing of the right neurons. In other words, the nose colour can be remembered by re-firing the same neurons that registered it in your brain in the first place. Our memory is therefore a physical thing from which information can be retrieved when, as it were, the right buttons are pushed. The late celebrated neurosurgeon, Wilder Penfield, was one of the first to figuratively press these buttons when he electrically stimulated areas of the brain to bring forth specific memories.

Because memory is a pattern of connections of physical substance, it is theoretically possible to transmit this pattern from the brain to a point elsewhere. But how?

Let's look at what's involved when information gets electronically moved from one storage facility to another. A good example, perhaps, is music. Your favorite record can be broadcast from New York and re-recorded, say, on the moon. The magnetic information on tape in the Big Apple is converted to voltage information in a wire, radiated electromagnetically to a lunar location, and re-recorded there on another tape. In this way, we can theoretically send information from any one place to any other place in the universe. Similarly, other types of data — graphics, for example — can also be transmitted and stored at a distance. This is done routinely by fax and computer.

It is clear, then, that earthlings have found ways to move certain kinds of information for instant retrieval at a distance, transmitting from point A and duplicating at B. Theoretically, this could apply to any pattern of information, even the memory patterns fixed in the brain. The entire memory of a brain at location A could conceivably be transmitted and stored again at any other location B.

This, then, is one of the basic ideas of the Saved Memory Hypothesis, namely: *there is a theoretical possibility of deploying memory patterns from the brain to some point outside the brain.* If achievable, then brain death and tissue decomposition at the end of life need have no more effect upon the preservation of someone's memory than would the destruction of a single recorded disk when a duplicate exists elsewhere. This brings us to the question: if the memory is transferred out of the brain, where is it transferred to?

## THE QUANTUM WORLD

We come now to the second basic idea of the Saved Memory Hypothesis, namely: *there is a place and medium somewhere in our universe (or system of universes) to which the memory patterns of the brain are transferred and preserved.* The place we suggest is an unseen world, contiguous with our own, governed by the principles of quantum mechanics. Call it a quantum world.

The quantum world is a world in which subatomic events take place in a milieu of nano-dimensions where our classical laws of space-time do not apply. And yet, as put by science-philosopher David Albert, quantum mechanics is the most precise mechanism for predicting the outcome of experiments on physical systems ever devised. Its laws are not easy to grasp, involving as they do the mathematics of superpositions, wave functions, wave-particle duality, indeterminacy, and other elusive concepts. We do not have the same intuitive feel for the quantum world as we do for the world described for us in terms of classical physics.

Although the mathematics of quantum theory are well understood, the principles behind the mathematics are not. For example, superstring theory (part of the quantum world) implies that physical reality may inhabit as many as 26 dimensions, where all the forces of nature, including gravity, are derived from the vibrations of tiny rips in space-time as small in comparison to a proton as a proton is compared to the size of the solar system.

Einstein, an early pioneer in the study of quantum energy, said in a famous quote that if quantum mechanics is right, then the world is crazy. Yet, as David Albert notes, no exceptions to their principles have ever been discovered, and nobody expects any. Nihls Bohr, the first person to describe the atom in terms of quanta, used to say that if you aren't confused by quantum physics, then you haven' t really understood it. Richard Feynmann, a pioneer of quantum electrodynamics (some of us saw him on TV explaining the explosion of the space-shuttle Columbia) said that *nobody* understood quantum mechanics.

Little wonder! Quantum theory conjures up multitudes of universes, and permits two contradictory statements to be true. It regards light as both wave and particle, and allows event A to influence event B, even though they are totally isolated from one another.

It is this weird world of multiple dimensions and bizarre effects that we nominate as a possible home for memory patterns transferred from our fleshy brains. In such a home, an unlimited number of 'saved' memories could lurk intimately and indefinitely among us at an unseen, subatomic level in our own universe.

Alternatively, the memories might exist in the quantum domains of other contiguous universes such as those envisaged by such cosmologists as Andrei Linde or Hugh Everett.

Linde, for example, postulates that our universe is only one of a large system of universes, all expanding and contracting in cycles. Each universe eventually squeezes down in a Big Crunch to a singularity which has no size at all. Here, all irregularities tend to get smoothed out, and information becomes lost.

But, according to Gerard t'Hooft of Utrecht University, quantum mechanics dictates that, in principle, information cannot be lost.

Well, there may be a way out of this conundrum whereby information, such as our saved memories, can avoid being crunched out of existence in a collapsing universe. Space-time, though it appears smooth at large scales, is said to have a foam-like submicroscopic structure containing many wormholes. It has been proposed that time travel by subatomic particles may take place through these holes (Deutsch & Lockwood, The Quantum Physics of Time Travel, Scientific American, March 1994). Perhaps the subatomic particles of memory patterns could escape through wormholes from an imploding universe and set up shop in a more stable one. If so, information would be saved, and Gerard t'Hooft would be spared the embarrassment of being wrong. For those who don't buy wormhole travel within or between universes, an alternative way of allowing our memories to escape the Big Crunch might be found in 'non-locality communication'. What is this? It is a phenomenon demonstrated by researchers in quantum mechanics that shows an event happening at point A can instantly influence point B, long before any signal could pass between the 2 points. This instant communication seems to occur no matter how far apart the points may be. Einstein called this poorly understood phenomenon 'spooky action at a distance'. By inference, any 2 points in the universe may be in instant communication with one another. Assuming that a variety of information patterns are communicable in this way, one may speculate that 'non-locality communication' might have potential for the translocation of saved memories from a collapsing universe to a safer one.

## ACCESSING THE MEMORY

In our presentation of the Saved Memory Hypothesis so far, we have postulated that memory survives death by translocation to a new site. But it is *Self* that we are interested in, not memory. Self has components of both memory and *consciousness*. Both are required for Self to survive. This leads us to the third postulate of the Saved Memory Hypothesis: *there is consciousness present to access transplanted memory at its new site.*

An obvious difficulty is evident here. We can conceptually move a static pattern like memory from A to B, just as we can move music encoded on magnetic tape from New York to the moon. But how does one move consciousness which is a dynamic process rather than a static pattern? In other words, even if you can take information in the brain and get it to a new storage site in sub atomic dimensions, what sort of process can we imagine that would make it function as consciousness? What is consciousness anyway?

According to respected researcher Francis Crick, consciousness is based solely on the interaction of neurons. Crick, who has spent many years investigating consciousness in his California lab, claims that, 'your joys and your sorrows, your memories and your ambitions, your sense of personal identity and free will, are in fact no more than the behavior of a vast assembly of nerve cells and their associated molecules.' Well, you can't scale down nerve cells to fit the size of the super-small dimensions of the quantum world. We must look to means other than nerve cells for the immortality of our self awareness.

Computer specialists, working in the field of artificial intelligence, are trying to build a device that shows consciousness.

Like Francis Crick, they regard brain consciousness as voltage changes in billions of nerves and their trillions of connections, and would like to emulate these. Whatever success they meet with, it is unlikely their device would fit the dimensions of the quantum world either.

Roger Penrose, a well known mathematician, physicist, and Nobel laureate, looks at consciousness from a different angle than that of Francis Crick or the artificial intelligence researchers. Penrose wonders how the rapid insights, leaps of intuition, and creativity of the brain (which he calls non-computational) could be fully accounted for by the limited number of nerve connections in the cerebral cortex. Penrose thinks quantum mechanics largely governs consciousness. He postulates that thoughts may exist in an infinite number of superposed states. When (in quantum mechanics jargon) the wave function collapses, one unique state clicks into the awareness envelope as a single thought.

Searching for a structure in the brain that could be responsible for the generation of quantum thought waves, Penrose, acting on a suggestion of fellow worker Stuart Hameroff, has cited microtubules as his candidate for quantum thought. These tiny protein structures are abundant in nerve cells as well as all other cells. However, microtubules, being part of the body, do not survive death, and they are far too large to be transmitted to a postmortem home in a quantum domain. It seems safe to conclude that microtubules, even if involved with the production of consciousness in the living brain, are not responsible for consciousness when the brain is dead.

Is there another way to achieve consciousness at the location of the saved memory without trying to scale down brain circuits? How about redesigning a new mechanism for consciousness that would fit at the new site? Would this be possible? If God can do it here every time he makes a brain, why not somewhere else? Granted, here he is working with DNA templates, but there may be other techniques available to Him. Rome can be reached by many roads. The octopus eye and the human eye are similar in structure and function, but they evolved along quite separate and distinct pathways. Can we not conceive of a device in nature that would be the functional equivalent of consciousness but created in a quantum domain from subatomic materials appropriate to that environment? This, indeed, is what the third postulate of the Saved Memory Hypothesis suggests could take place: *the duplicated memory is accessed in its new milieu by a consciousness mechanism physically different to that of our brain.* Consciousness, unlike static memory patterns, is a functional process that, if modeled on the brain, could not conceivably be compacted into the nano-dimensions of the quantum world. It appears obvious that, if we continue to exist beyond death in a quantum domain, then God has come up with a design other than the brain for consciousness.

We have, up to this point, looked at three components of a hypothesis for immortality. We must include a fourth part if this idea is to make any sense.

## CONTINUOUS TRANSFER

People change from day to day, from moment to moment, so our lives are made up of many Selves. Which Self is the candidate for immortality? This leads us to the fourth postulate of the Saved Memory Hypothesis: *memory patterns are translocated continuously from the brain.* In other words, all our Selves are saved. What is the significance of this postulate?

In the living brain, the memory may be regarded as a repository in which every event, every emotion, every thought and feeling experienced during life has registered, however briefly, in precisely the same detail as that in which it was originally sensed. And yet, only the smallest fraction of all this information is captured by the memory for more than the briefest instant. Most of what we experience cannot be recalled from one moment to the next. For example, how much of what happens to us during each second of the day can we recall at bedtime? How much of each minute of our lives do we distinctly remember at life's end? Of the total input, we retain only a few isolated, faded recollections that have been distorted by time and are in no way comparable, even under hypnotic recall, to the rich detail of the original experience. Unlike magnetic tape which can store every sound wave of a well-recorded musical performance with extraordinary fidelity, the memory in the brain is a storage device capable of retaining only sporadic events in rough approximation.

Thus, when we arrive at the point of death, we remember little of our past lives. If we have suffered brain injury, we remember even less. The degrading of the rich stream of data leaves us with just a shadowy impression of our past life.

For post-mortem existence, this would not do. To prevent, therefore, the transmission of a deficient and incomplete memory, the writer, in his exalted position as creator of plausible or implausible scenarios, is able to imagine that the memory might be relocated from the brain by incremental transfer or, better still, *continuous* transfer during life. All information, as it registers in the brain, is at the same time transmitted to its alternate site. In this way, there is no detail of our past experience that is lost.

Looking at computers, we note that after information is entered, the data may be lost or degraded for a variety of reasons including, for example, power failure. To guard against such a loss, we 'save' the data from time to time, perhaps by transfer to hard disk, during the course of operation. In this way, added information is incrementally allocated to permanent storage where there is little danger of future loss.

When we think about transfer of data from the brain, we may imagine God, seated at his divine mainframe, punching the save button or even leaning on it! In this way, the information existing in the brain at every microsecond during life would be preserved in all its original detail at the new storage site.

If such is the case, then we can propose a re-animated memory after death with the potential for recalling, even reliving, life with absolute accuracy, eliminating any distinction between actual earthly existence and its virtual recall in the post-mortem memory. We would smell, taste, see, hear, and feel as we did before because *nothing* is lost or degraded. We would feel that we were using our muscles and exercising our free will as we had done in life. We might not even be aware that we were recycling memories, and in fact be under the impression that we were still alive.

**RECALL AFTER ALZHEIMER'S**

The concept of the transfer of information continuously as it reaches the brain instead of at death only means that the loss of memory when natural degradation, disease, and injury take their toll upon the living brain would be a phenomenon of life only. With continuous transfer, information that was received and processed at any time during life would be saved regardless of what happened to the brain after the event. Thus, falling victim to Alzheimer's disease, for example, which would wipe out the living memory, would not in any way affect information that had already been transferred. The living person who loses his recall would, in effect, be given everything back again at death. We have now presented the 4 elements of the Saved Memory Hypothesis. In summary, they are:

*1. There is a theoretical possibility of deploying memory patterns from the brain to some point outside the brain.*

*2. There is a place and medium to which the memory patterns of the brain may be transferred and preserved.*

*3. The explanted memory is accessed after death by an activity similar to consciousness.*

*4. Memory patterns are transferred continuously from the brain during the course of life.*

How true is all this? A hypothesis, obviously, is only a guess that has to be tested before it can be said to have any validity. With regard to the 4 elements of the Saved Memory Hypothesis, we have extrapolated from knowns into the realm of the unknown.

a) We know it's possible to transmit a stored pattern from A to

B (for example, a recorded version of Ravel's Bolero). We have yet to test whether brain memory is, indeed, transmissible. Since it is a stored pattern, the possibility exists.

b) We know from experimental evidence that the quantum world is real. It remains to be tested whether or not it could accommodate a memory pattern relocated from the brain.

c) We know that consciousness is created every time a brain is made. We don't know if a facsimile could exist and function together with memory in quantum dimensions.

The knowns constitute a 3-pronged base from which the ideas of the Saved Memory Hypothesis have been launched. The unknowns are the hypothetical elements that remain to be tested. As science continues to reveal to us how our world works, a means for testing these unproved elements may materialize. Meanwhile, we speculate.

**SPECULATIONS**

*A new body*: Even if our Self lived among the quarks and leptons of a quantum world, we would find that our body couldn't. For one thing, it wouldn't fit. For another, nothing would work because the physical laws are quite different there. Of what use would arms, legs, eyes, and ears be to an homunculus existing, for instance, in the recesses of an atom? If the post-mortem Self needs a body at all, it might approximate the size of a light photon, have no recognizable shape, and be both particle and wave.

*The old memory*: If we don't like what we find when the grim reaper escorts us to our new abode, we can cop out by taking refuge in earthly memories. The Saved Memory Hypothesis holds that the memory of our life on Earth can be relived with the same reality and detail that we experienced in life. We will be able to choose, or not, whether to relive these memories, just as we can choose in life whether we wish to sleep and dream, or stay awake and have new experiences.

*New dimensions*: It is alleged that the quantum world may contain up to 26 dimensions. Humans are used to only 3 space dimensions, and one time. Although the 26 dimensions are mathematical abstractions, so too at a fundamental level are the space-time dimensions in which we live, yet they seem quite real to us. For anyone timid about new experience, the altered, radically different environment may take some getting used to.

*Resequenced memories*: The Saved Memory Hypothesis, although conceived to suggest the possibility of Self survival is, by itself, merely a formula for recycling the past. But reruns become a bore. Even if it was not apparent that one was reliving a former life, the business of endlessly re-experiencing bygone events seems pointless to our logical brains. However, there is some scope for variation. For example, one can change the order of the components in the remembered series, like an editor altering a film by removing some frames and splicing in others. This happens in dreams where past experiences and impressions are linked together in altered sequences that can be compellingly realistic to the dreamer but have little relation to the events of past life. Thus, we may easily find ourselves flying in our dreams without the benefit of wings which would be impossible if we were awake. Or we can imagine a dead musician rearranging remembered pitches and orchestral sounds in altered sequences to produce new compositions and performances that he might consider fresh rather than recycled.

Yet, even with the flexibility provided by juggling the order of past events, it is hard to anticipate any such resequencing procedures with much enthusiasm. It is true that we could take comfort in a strong memory link with our past life. However, the fascination we found in that life was the moment to moment challenge of change and new experience. What are the prospects for this after death?

If the postulated environment for our translocated memories includes the dimension of time, then the potential for new events would exist there as well as here, and the possibility for interaction between the reanimated memory and the new environment could occur as it did in life.

*Other people*: When, and if, we survive death, shall we be

alone? Not likely. Nature abhors uniqueness. If one memory can be translocated from the brain to a new environment, presumably others can also.

On earth, people (as the song says) need people. Humans mate, work, love, fight, and interact with one another in a thousand different ways. Only a hermit envies Robinson Crusoe on his desert island. But human interaction requires communication. If there is a society of post-mortem Selves without tongues, vocal chords, or other signaling devices, one wonders how they might communicate with each other.

*Conclusion*: In the musings of this section, under *speculations*, we have imagined some of the conditions one might encounter in a post-mortem world. This, of course, is fanciful speculation because no real answers are available. Although speculation may be intriguing, thought provoking, even comforting, its value stops there. To have real answers, we must first construct a hypothesis, then test it. A testable hypothesis will be built on a foundation of fact, and, as previously explained to the reader, this is the approach that has been followed in formulating the Saved Memory Hypothesis. The author proposes that the Saved Memory Hypothesis rests on far firmer ground than the speculations listed above which, nevertheless, have a valid place in any discussion of 'life after death.'

Let's turn, then, to the subject of Self since this is the key to any thought of survival after death.

# THE SELF

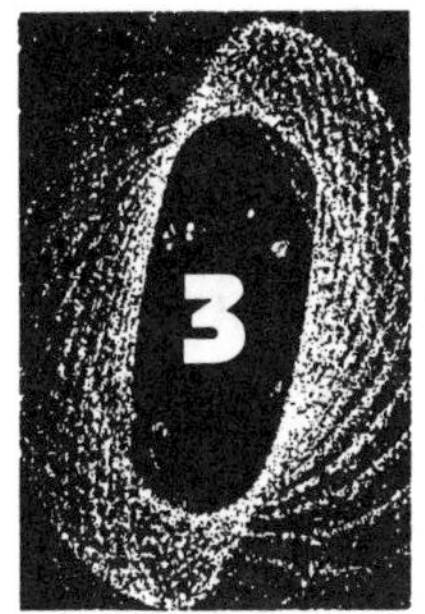


The 5 1/2 or so billion people presently on earth that use the pronoun 'I' in their daily conversation are referring to their body, ('I am tall') or their mind ('I am happy'). Everyone knows what the body is, but who can define the mind, or Self as we will call it? Is this entity, the Self, separate from the body, part of the body, or a process going on within the body?

When the French philosopher Rene Descartes tried to come to grips with the concept of Self, he became more and more confused until he began to seriously doubt that he, himself, existed. Ultimately, he concluded that he did exist because, in order to doubt, something must be there to do the doubting ('I think, therefore I am').

But Descartes' conclusion doesn't help define the Self. The Concise Oxford Dictionary says that the Self means a person's, or thing's, own individuality or essence. What does that tell us? It merely substitutes one nebulous term for another. We must go further.

When Descartes wrote about this subject, he knew nothing of the detailed architecture of the brain. He couldn't even guess at the structures that support components of Self like consciousness and memory. Today, centuries later, neuroscientists are beginning to correlate these mental events with patterns of nerve impulses in the brain. Modern tools such as positron emission tomography, magnetic resonance imaging, and radioautography help them do this. Using objective ways of studying the brain, it should be possible someday to break down the Self into its hard-wired components.

## THE SELF AND THE BRAIN

The awareness of Self in this world relies on a functioning brain. Our limbs may be amputated, our organs transplanted, our senses lost, but as long as our brain functions properly, the sense of Self is expected to be there. If brain function is impaired, however, as by deep coma or anesthetic, the sense of Self disappears. We no longer know we exist.

I remember as a boy holding the back of my hand up to a mirror and thinking: 'Is this strange looking object really a part of me? Has it anything to do with my Self?' The longer I stared at it, the more foreign it seemed to become, until it appeared positively alien. I felt that my sense of Self would not be diminished if the hand were lost.

The hand has no apparent sense of Self. Although each of its cells contains information in its DNA to create a whole body, brain and all, there is nevertheless no evidence of Self until a brain is formed. If Frankenstein, in his macabre exploits, had removed a brain from its cranium and hooked it up to a blood perfusion apparatus, he might have expected the brain to retain its sense of Self. The separated body, of course, would not.

## THE SELF AND THE SENSES

Do the senses play a role in the creation of our self-awareness? Indeed, they have an indispensable function. To continue for a moment in a macabre mode, let us suppose that Dr. Frankenstein, functioning as an obstetrician, has delivered a baby and, at the moment of birth, cut all of the nerves from the eyes, ears, and other senses so that no information went to the newborn infant's brain. Would we expect such a child, if it survived without being able to see, hear, smell, taste, or feel, to grow up knowing anything about its surroundings? Would such a person, with no sensory input after birth, have a sense of Self?

We would guess not. An infant without sensory experience after birth would have no significant impressions, images, or concepts whatsoever upon which to base mental awareness. It is interesting that the brain circuits we are born with are 'plastic', not hard-wired. They undergo changes when we leave the womb and meet the outside world. It is information from the world, flooding into the brain from the senses, that brings about changes in the neural circuits. Nerve synapses alter in number and location, axons sprout new endings, dendritic arbors are remodeled, post-synaptic receptors change in number, genes are activated, and new proteins made. Worldly experience, in other words, results in physical changes to cerebral nerves and their connections. These physical changes are involved in the formation of memory, consciousness, and perception of Self. They are based on sensory input. Without the senses, the brain would be left as it presumably was before birth containing virtually no information, memory, or conscious perception of Self.

**THE SELF AND MEMORY**

When sensory signals reach the brain, what happens to them? Well, let's suppose we're watching a dog cross the street. Light reflected from its brown coat falls upon our retina, causing electro-chemical impulses to be sent via various relays to the visual cortex of our brain where the impulses are processed, rerouted, and ultimately find their way through a multitude of nerve connections to a memory network. We now have a retrievable image in our brain of the dog crossing the street.

Similarly, other information communicated to our brain by our other senses does not simply enter the brain and then disappear. The information is recorded there for varying periods of time, and can be selectively accessed for future use. As put by neuroscientists A. Damasio and H. Damasio (Scientific American, September '92), the brain holds a record of the neural activity that takes place in the sensory and motor cortices during interaction with a given object. The records are patterns of synaptic connections that can recreate the separate sets of activity that define an object or event. Many anatomically separate and widely distributed neuron ensembles fire simultaneously and reconstruct previous patterns of mental activity. Related events and concepts — shapes, colors, trajectories in space and time, and pertinent body movements and reactions — can be reactivated together.

Some sensory information is retained in the memory for a long while, whereas other data, having less priority, are remembered for a much shorter time. Hence, we refer to 'long term' and 'short term' memory. The image of a dog crossing the street will likely be stored in the long term memory if some remarkable event, such as the dog being hit by a car, increases the relevance of the incident to the observer. Otherwise, the affair will merge with all the other miscellaneous happenings of the day and soon be forgotten.

Kandel and Hawkins (Scientific American, September '92) have noted that storage of initial information (short term memory) lasts minutes to hours and involves changes in the strength of existing synaptic connections. The long term changes (weeks to months) are stored at the same site, but they require the activation of genes, the synthesis of new proteins, and the growth of new connections. The hippocampus appears to be a temporary depository for long term memory (weeks to months) after which it transfers the information to relevant areas of the cerebral cortex for more permanent storage, from where it is expressed through the working memory ('the blackboard of the mind') of the prefrontal cortex.

What has the Self, which is what we are concerned about here, got to do with long and short term memory? Simply this: short term memory gives us a transitory recording of information, perhaps only for the briefest instant, and the Self relates to it only temporarily. The millions of separate items of information sent by our senses to the brain are soon beyond recall, and are important in contributing to the sense of awareness only at the immediate moment of reception. In contrast, the events more permanently recorded in our memory — the long term memory — build up a lasting image of our Self.

Now, it is important to the Saved Memory Hypothesis to ask the question: could a person with *intact memory*, but with all information from the 5 senses cut off, be fully conscious and have a sense of Self? Why not? As long as there is a rich store of information already in the brain to think about, to be aware of, to manipulate, acquired before the senses were shut down, then the cognitive processes would presumably remain active. Our identity would not be lost. This point is fundamental to the Saved Memory Hypothesis which postulates that we retain our memories, but not our senses, after death.

In view of the apparent association between Self and memory, it makes sense to ask what happens to the Self in a victim of amnesia. If Jane Brown, for example, suffers amnesia after a traumatic automobile accident, is her sense of Self, allegedly tied to memory, diminished? If she can't recall her name, address, work, or friends, is she less aware of herself as a person? No. Jane Brown' s sense of Self would be intact because:

1. Her sensory input is not impaired.
2. Her memory of events since the amnesia onset is normal.
3. Her memory before amnesia is only partially lost. She still remembers how to walk, talk, read, compute, and so on.

The sense of Self in the amnesia victim is alive and well, unlike that of the person we imagined that was deprived of sensory information from birth by Dr. Frankenstein.

## THE SELF AND CONSCIOUSNESS

The Self cannot exist without information retrieved from the memory and senses by the mental activity we call consciousness. It is presumed that we are not dealing with a mystical, abstract phenomenon when we talk about consciousness, but rather with a process involving interconnected nerve pathways activated by electrical impulses and chemical neurotransmitters. This mental activity may scan the memory somewhat at random, as in the free association of daydreaming, or by systematic search as in directed thought. The process of consciousness somehow selects, compares, and manipulates data from the memory, and integrates it with the stream of sensory input. The result is the Self.

The integrity of consciousness, as noted earlier in this chapter, is dependent on normal brain function. If we consider the deeply comatose patient, we note that conscious activity is dormant and the sense of Self absent, even though the anatomical connections of memory remain intact. In the more extreme case where the brain is permanently destroyed by death, then sensory input, its structural record in the memory, and conscious activity will of course cease to exist in this world. We would no longer be able to depend on the brain for our awareness.

In summary, we have concluded that the Self is made up of the following:

1. Sensory input
2. Structural record in the brain of this input
3. Conscious retrieval and processing of the input

## THE ROLE OF THE SELF

The Self is the captain of the body, plotting and steering the course for survival. All the parts of our body, such as muscles, glands, nerves, and blood, function together automatically to support life, but these parts would not last long in higher animals without the Self. Every cell in our body needs food, and it is the Self that contrives to gather the food and get it to our mouth. Thinking animals need to protect themselves from dangers that continually threaten their existence, and this protection is coordinated by their analytical brain under the direction of Self. It is with the motivation and guidance of Self that humans have learned to cultivate crops, invent the wheel, discover fire, and explore space.

## THE SELF IN OTHER SPECIES

The Self is indispensable, not only for humans, but also for other higher animals. The more developed the central nervous system becomes during evolution, the greater is the role played by the Self in the survival of the organism. Thus, the Self is more important to a human's survival than it is, say, to an oyster where reflex response has a greater role in determining behavior.

Do all living organisms have at least some sense of Self? The question is moot. An animal with a well developed brain may easily be imagined to have an awareness of Self when its complex analytical behavior and capacity for social intercourse is observed. These attributes depend on thought processes analogous to our own. One has only to witness a guide dog steering its blind companion across a busy street to receive the impression that the dog's brain has the memory, retrieval, and associative mechanisms which can produce an awareness of Self.

On the other hand, it would seem funny if a much simpler form of life, say a blood cell or a virus particle, would have any sense of Self. Such organisms do not possess a central nervous system or brain. They do not have any visible means of receiving or analyzing complex sensory stimuli such as those received through our sophisticated sensory receptors. They rely, as far as we know, upon simple chemical or tactile stimuli to elicit responses, with no switching or central processing that could produce thought. A blood cell may migrate to a region of infection and engulf bacteria in response to chemical signals deployed from the infection site, but it is improbable that it could think about what it was doing as would, for instance, a tiger stalking its prey. One presumes that the tiger has a sense of Self, but the blood cell does not.

But can we be certain that a simple unicellular organism, such as a blood cell or an amoeba, is without a sense of Self? Isn't it possible that the organism could think by some means or structure that is not evident to us?

We can be certain, of course, of nothing, but the probability that an amoeba can think seems negligible.

Can a horse fly? We don't think so because it doesn't have wings, rotor blades, rockets, or a belly full of helium. One can always guess that a horse may have a hidden mechanism that could make it take off and soar like a bird. However, our experience tells us that the likelihood is vanishingly small, and we dismiss the idea without a second thought.

Similarly, the possibility of an amoeba being able to think also approaches zero. Not only is there no detectable means to support thought, but there is no evident requirement for thinking. Unlike a higher animal, the amoeba can survive, multiply, and do whatever an amoeba does without the encumbrance of mental logic.

Which animals, then, have a sense of Self, and which do not?

Life covers a wide range of biological complexity. For example, a virus in its simplest form consists of a single nucleic acid chain surrounded by a few protein molecules. About the most it can do is reproduce itself with the help of its cell host. In contrast, the complexity of a human being is dazzling, involving trillions of interacting cells whose functions go far beyond simple replication. Is there a line of division somewhere between virus and human where it may be said: 'On this side of the line there is Self, on that side there is none?' We do not know where to draw such a line, and assume by default that Self exists to different degrees in different animals according to their complexity.

What about differences in the sense of Self between animals of similar complexity, say the human and the whale, but which differ as to size, shape, function, behavior, and environment? Do these two mammals have a sense of Self that is species dependent? One presumes they do. The human Self and the whale Self occupy two strikingly different bodies living in habitats that require one to swim, the other to walk. The man sells insurance, plays golf, watches television with the kids, drives his car. The whale has a different set of priorities, interests, and challenges shaped by its different milieu, body, and brain. Since the Self has evolved to help the body cope with its surroundings, and since the bodies and surroundings of whale and human are so different, we expect that the sense of awareness in the two animals is different also.

In summary, we conclude that:

1. The degree of sense of Self in an animal relates to the complexity of its central nervous system.

2. Self awareness directs higher forms of life toward survival, but is not a requirement for the survival of lower forms.

3. Organisms without brains possess no detectable structure that could provide awareness of Self as we know it.

4. The sense of Self is species related.

## THE SELF AND MATURATION

What happens to the Self as we grow older? As an adult we have an acute sense of Self, as a two-day-old infant a foggier one, and as a one-month-old embryo presumably close to none. If we extend our look from the single cell that started us on the road of existence to a sick and senile person with dull senses and impaired brain function at the far end of life, there will be a curve of awareness starting at zero, rising to a peak, and then declining. These degrees form a continuum with no particular point that separates the presence of Self from its absence.

The earliest beginnings of the Self are presumed to appear when the embryo's senses and central nervous system start to function. We can imagine that the initial sensory stimuli reaching the embryonic brain are rudimentary, consisting perhaps of nerve transmissions from joints and muscles providing information about the position and movement of limbs. Later, sound waves from outside the womb begin to be perceived through the embryo's auditory apparatus.

When the baby is born, a quantum leap occurs as the 5 senses kick in with information from a vastly enriched environment with which the body can now interact. The learning process starts in earnest. The passive existence of the fetus bathed in protective amniotic fluid has been superseded by the shock of birth, and the sense of Self begins its rapid course of development which will direct the newborn child in the business of survival.

As noted earlier, the barrage of sensory signals which are selectively registered in the memory is the cause for the changes in our perception of Self. As new experiences occur in our progression from infancy through adolescence, adulthood, and old age, our sense of Self and the way we direct our body to survive is continuously modified. Even during periods of minimal sensory input, the information already in the memory may be recombined and manipulated by the brain over the course of time to form new insights that may subtly alter the nature of Self. When old age finally catches up with us, if we find that our senses don't work as well, our memories are foggy, and our mental discrimination has lost its former sharpness, we may find a corresponding impairment in the ability of the Self to direct the body. The Self is not what it was yesterday, nor will it be tomorrow what it is today.

Another factor in our lives besides the passage of time which can alter the sense of Self is disease or brain injury. Suppose, for example, that you are temporarily in a deep coma. You lose your sense of awareness. Upon recovery, your awareness is restored. Whenever brain physiology is sufficiently disturbed regardless of the cause, the sense of Self will be altered until the derangement is corrected or compensated for. Thus, self perception may be changed in patients experiencing the hallucinations or delusions of meningitis, encephalitis, high fever, or schizophrenia. Other agents affecting self perception are mood altering drugs, anesthetics, Alzheimer's plaques, syphilitic lesions, cerebral palsy, congenital deformities, trauma, toxins, and so on.

What happens to the Self when we are asleep?

If the reader succumbs to drowsiness while reading these lines, the sense of Self will lose some of its sharpness. If he or she actually falls into a dreamless sleep, it will be totally lost. In dreams, there will be a sense of Self, but it will be different. Our dreams are formed from the shifting imagery and components of past experience, and it is within such a world of passive memory manipulation that the dreamer's Self is forged. The Self in the dream continues to direct the body, but the body is imaginary. Further, the dreaming person doesn't know that he or she is asleep and that experiences, however real they may seem, are generated within the brain alone. Someone who is awake, however, is quite convinced, for obscure reasons, that he or she is not dreaming or reliving past events resurrected from his or her memory.

## DUPLICATION OF THE SELF

Bodies can be replicated. We are all familiar with identical twins that come from a single egg. We also know that the DNA in every cell of our body can theoretically produce a duplicate body. In fact, you and I have the potential for an army of identical body replicas. Not twins, not quintuplets, but thousands exactly like us stretching to the horizon.

But what about Self? Is there a DNA template that replicates the Self along with the body?

No. The Self is essentially synthesized by events that occur after birth. Although it depends on brain architecture and therefore on DNA, the Self is synthesized from information that is subsequently recorded there. Each individual's experiences are unique. Therefore, his or her Self is unique.

To illustrate, imagine 3 identical body replicas named Tom, Bill, and Dave. Tom goes to a concert, Bill to work at the factory, and Dave to war. Each receives sensory data peculiar to himself. The information stored in each memory is unique. The result: each of the 3 identical bodies would have non-identical Selves shaped by contrasting experience. This is evident when we note the differences of behavior shown by identical twins. Even though there is a duplication of genes, there is no duplication of Self.

Let's go back to Frankenstein's lab, where we find the doctor, as usual, up to no good. He has produced 3 body clones and exposed them to precisely the same sensory input from the moment of creation. Each clone, in other words, has received the same visual, auditory, gustatory, olfactory, and tactical impulses as the others in exactly the same sequence and strength. The information in all 3 memory banks is identical. Would Frankenstein detect 3 identical Selves in his 3 clones?

The answer must logically be yes. Since each clone has a body, brain, and memorized information identical to that of the other two, one would expect the behavior of the 3 to be identical. This means that if the Self has no mystical or supernatural component, the identity known as "I" would apply interchangeably and without distinction to any of the 3 clones.

Now, Frankenstein calls his 3 creations to him and says: "Look here, fellows, I can only afford to feed one of you, not three. Who will volunteer for termination?"

Each clone, motivated by a personal sense of identity and drive for survival, urges upon Dr. Frankenstein his partisan point of view that the others, not he, should be terminated.

"I don't want to die," shout the 3 clones.

"But you are all identical," points out the exasperated doctor. Frankenstein forthwith ends the argument by letting the clones draw straws for the privilege of living.

With few exceptions, the survival of other Selves seems less important to us than the continued existence of our own Self. We call someone a hero or heroine who voluntarily lays down his or her life that another Self may live.

# WHY HUMANS INVENTED RELIGION

## FEAR OF DEATH

Humans run from death with the same enthusiasm that a mouse runs from a cat. A healthy fear of death is necessary for both humans and mice to survive and multiply. The seed is spread only by an individual that lives long enough to become a parent. I am thankful to my ancestors that they had a fear of death.

But in man's makeup, there is a refinement that sets him apart from other animals. Because man has a brain that is more complex and better adapted for abstract thought than other brains, he may be the only organism that can consciously predict, or foresee, his own death. He notes that the trees around him soon perish and rot, or burn, or are made into lumber. He sees the rice and corn in his garden broken down in his intestines and expelled as non-living excrement. He watches animals devouring one another and knows that they will also be converted into intestinal fecal matter. When man's cerebral cortex reflects upon these things, it becomes evident to him that all life on this planet eventually dies and is returned to nature's common pool of atoms and molecules. He is consciously aware that he is very much a part of this natural process, and that therefore he is also destined to die.

There is one clear consequence that emerges from this pattern of events that cannot help but impress man unfavorably. It is the fact that there is no discernible continuity between the entity that was once alive and the inanimate parts that are scattered about in death. When man thinks about this, he finds it profoundly disturbing. He knows that he, himself, forms part of the Earth' s family of living organisms that inevitably die, and that his body awaits a fate no different than that of other organisms that have ceased to live. He wonders what will happen to his sense of self under such circumstances. Logic shouts to him that, because his sense of awareness depends on his brain, this awareness must cease when his brain is destroyed. So, when he looks into his crystal ball for an image of the future, there is something critical that is missing. Himself! Death has seemingly brought about his annihilation.

Man is thus saddled with a permanent and disturbing conflict. On the one hand, his unique intellect tells him that death cannot be avoided. On the other hand, the powerful instinct for self preservation that he shares with other animals propels him to a 'fight or flight' response in a struggle to avoid death. As he nears middle age, he becomes more aware of his approaching end, and his apprehension commonly increases. Carl Jung, the pioneering psychiatrist, has said that he never had a patient over forty that was not bothered by the fear of death. How, then, is man able to cope with this potentially devastating conflict between the instinct for survival and the anticipation of death? How can he get through the day without, as they say, being driven up the wall by this crisis that has no apparent solution?

## DISTRACTION FROM THOUGHTS OF DEATH

The evolution of man's brain has provided it with a superb device for removing most of the sting from the anticipation of death. If you are an 'average' person, you think about death very little. You, your family, your friends and acquaintances, all go about the hectic business of life with an intensity that leaves little room for thoughts about a distant end. Whether watching TV, playing a sport, enjoying a hobby, or bringing home the daily bread, man is customarily engrossed exclusively in what he is doing at any given moment. His mind is distracted from other reflections, especially those concerning a remote death.

For example, as the reader reads these lines, he is probably fully absorbed in an attempt to understand the meaning of the author's words. If he is interested in what is written, it is not likely that his attention will be diverted by random intrusions. The TV may blare, the kids may shout, the dog may bark, but he continues to give his full attention to the printed page. In the same way, a *yogi* in deep meditation while seated on a bed of nails may be mentally oblivious to the painful indentations in his skin. This indicates the extraordinary capacity of the human brain to concentrate on one thing at a time. We have here a highly efficient mechanism in man's brain that is used to escape from the ever present, underlying conflict between the animal instinct for survival and the human knowledge of impending death. Nature has, as usual, done her evolutionary work exceeding well, for the challenges in man's life provide him with an unending series of tasks that keep his conscious thoughts far removed from the morbid contemplation of personal annihilation. He spends the day obtaining food, shelter, clothing, safety, and amusement, and the demanding details of these occupations distract him from troubling thoughts of his mortality. But the system of distraction is not perfect. Hiding from all thoughts of death is not one hundred percent efficient. Morbid reminders, never fully suppressed, are ready to jump forth particularly in times of sickness, danger, depression, inactivity, or random reflection. The conflict between survival and death has only been covered up, not eliminated. Like the Dutch boy with his finger in the dike, the problem is held at bay as long as the hole is plugged. If the boy walks away, or the brain's concentration is overpowered, the flood waters gush forth ready to do their damage unopposed. For this reason, man needs help from other sources to get through the day without being upset by images of his own demise.

## INVENT A SOLUTION

If you don't have the solution to a problem, invent one, and convince yourself that it works. You may not have changed anything except your mind, but a change of mind may be of vital importance in special circumstances. This is the case when facing death without the power to prevent it. If one thinks that one has the solution, then the quality of life is much improved regardless of whether or not the belief is right.

Man finds himself in this situation when he is forced by the evidence around him to acknowledge the inevitability of his own end. He cannot find a solution to the problem, so he wills one. His solution is to *deny* that he will be annihilated. He accepts the logic of his brain that tells him his body will be destroyed at death, but he refuses to admit to the loss of his self awareness as an accompaniment of death. He is able to deny this by creating a system of beliefs in his mind that promises the survival of self awareness despite the loss of the body. In other words, he convinces himself of the existence of supernatural powers that will provide the means for the continuance of the abstraction he calls spirit or soul after his body is disassembled.

## TEMPERING THE FEAR OF DEATH

Enter religion into the life of man. Religion is a means by which mankind stems the flood of anxiety and fear that tends to gush forth when, figuratively speaking, the Dutch boy pulls his finger out of the dike. On such occasions man may, if his religious convictions are strong, lean on them to help him cope with thoughts of death. The future does not appear to hold any mysterious terrors for one who feels certain that his identity is fated, not merely to survive death, but to ultimately prosper in a new and blissful realm. Depending on the degree to which he is convinced of this, the religious person may pursue his worldly tasks without intrusive thoughts of death. A religious man's concern about an uncertain future over which he has no evident control tends to dissolve, not because the problem is solved, but because of faith in the belief that there is no problem.

## KNOWING THE UNKNOWN

People assume that there must be a cause for every effect,

and they want to know what the causes are. They seek tirelessly to find them, and if they are unsuccessful, they feel ill at ease. When prehistoric man saw lightning flash in the sky and could not understand the reason, he decided that lightning must be the angry expression of an awesome superhuman controlling power. In the absence of a more rational explanation, this one had to serve. Since those earlier times, science has come up with a less spectacular explanation for lightning, namely, the discharge of static electricity built up in turbulent cumulonimbus clouds. But not withstanding science, modern man is still tempted to evoke the operation of a supernatural agent when he cannot find a more obvious cause. For example, his brain tells him that he and the universe must have been brought into existence by some agent which, to his considerable frustration, he cannot identify. Therefore, like ancient man before him, he invokes a mystic power as the cause. This human recognition of a superhuman controlling power is, according to The Concise Oxford Dictionary, the definition of religion. But does not today's Big Bang theory of creation undermine the concept of God as creator of the universe? Not at all. Man speculates that God, as the primeval agent, must have been present to engineer the Big Bang in the first place. As in the case of lightning, however, science will no doubt continue undeterred to search for more detail to supplement this divine view of creation.

## OTHER NEEDS ARE MET

Religion, or belief in a superhuman controlling power, had to be invented to fill two human needs. These have been mentioned and, in summary, are:

1. The need to believe in some kind of existence after death.
2. The need to know the cause for every effect.

There are other needs of man that are met by religion. For example, when we are young, if we should cut our finger or bruise our knee, we run to our parents in fear and pain for comfort and reassurance. We also rely on our mother or father to provide favors, gifts, love, and guidance. When we outgrow the ability of our parents to satisfy these needs, we turn to religion. Many of us refer to God as God the Father, and He fulfills the role of a divine surrogate parent, replacing the human one. Thus the adult, who may no longer be able to lean on human parental love, may seek guidance and protection through religion.

Another obvious benefit provided by religion is the establishment of a code of moral values that promotes harmony between men. We see examples of this in the ten commandments handed down to Moses, the five Precepts of Buddha's eight-fold path to Nirvana, the four *yoga's* of Hinduism, and the ethical order of Confucius.

The keystone to any religion is *faith*. Faith is belief without evidence. We can have faith in the existence of anything, providing that we can convince ourselves of its truth. Columbus told the North American natives that he could make the moon disappear from the sky. Some believed him simply on the authority of his word; they had faith. When the eclipse took place, their faith was justified, although not because of anything Columbus did. Faith may be well, or ill, founded, and it is often not clear which. It is said that the Christian martyrs, as they filed into the gaming arena to be mauled by starving lions, often sang and cried out joyously in anticipation of an imminent ascent to Heaven. This is faith in action.

Without the keystone of faith firmly in place, the arch of any religious belief will fall. It could not be any other way. Religion, by definition, is supernatural. Because it is abstract, intangible, and subjective, man has never been able to demonstrate its 'superhuman controlling power' by what he regards as objective proof. He therefore has to convince himself, by the force of his will and his need, that such a superhuman controlling power exists. He has been largely successful in doing exactly this, and his conviction is called faith. By keeping his faith solidly in place, the arch of his religion stands firm. This usually requires substantial reinforcement, and there are many methods by which this reinforcement may be obtained.

## RELIGION NEEDS TOOLS

Little Mary is getting baptized. The Reverend Smith, suitably robed, stoops down and dabs water on her forehead or, if the ceremony has a more dynamic format, immerses Mary in a tub. Everyone in the small congregation smiles happily as the infant cries in protest. The bathing of Jesus by John the Baptist has been re-enacted, and the betting is that little Mary's soul now has a better than even chance of ultimately making it to, and through, Heaven's Pearly Gates. Little Mary's family and friends know that the requirements of their religion and of their God have been duly met, and all, for the moment, is well with the world.

The ceremony of baptism is symbolic, and symbols, as we know, are a prominent feature of all religions. This is hardly surprising. If a person feels that his present and future welfare are intimately tied to his relationship with a supernatural being, he obviously considers that it is in his interest to keep that relationship alive and, as it were, cooking. A relationship with an abstract entity has, by definition, no objective criteria to give form to the abstraction, no sensory information to give it shape or substance. It can neither be seen, heard, nor touched. To keep such a nebulous relationship steadily in view is not easy. 'Out of sight, out of mind,' as the saying goes. Symbols or reminders, therefore, have great utility in religion. They remind the religious person of the relationship he wishes to nurture, of the abstraction he wishes to keep before him, and his attention is never allowed to stray very far or for very long.

Now, let us watch some tools of religion at work. First, observe a Muslim as he prays kneeling on the ground facing in the direction of Mecca, the Holy City where the famed messenger of God, Mohammed, was born. It is noon. The worshiper prayed first when he got up that morning, and he will pray again in the afternoon, after sunset, and before going to bed. His prayers are expressions of praise, gratitude, and supplication to his god, Allah. Through this ceremony of prayer, he is reminded of Allah at least five times a day. His prayer thus serves as an important tool in the preservation and strengthening of his relationship with his God.

If we now shift the scene to a Roman Catholic cathedral, we can observe some tools, this time, of Christianity at work. A worshiper rises from her *knees, rosary* in hand, and proceeds from her *pew* to the *altar* where a *priest* offers her *bread* and *wine* from a holy *Host* and *Chalice* while a *replica* of Christ looks down from the *Cross.* One or more of these symbols and reminders will help her to focus her attention on God.

If we look in turn upon a follower of Judaism, we will probably agree that he is unlikely to forget Yahweh, the Creator, while he fasts during the High Holiday of Yom Kippur. His stomach, which in this case is a tool of religion, should remind him effectively.

Religious symbols and reminders may take many forms which include ceremonies, holidays, rituals, musical performances, dances, chants, scriptures, buildings, tombs, paintings, sculptures, and artifacts of all kinds. What would our concept of the Roman Catholic religion be, we may wonder, without its Sacraments, its cathedral services, its Pope, cardinals, bishops, and priests, its Bible, its crosses, rosaries, and other reminders of biblical figures and events. These are all tools to turn the attention of the devout Christian to thoughts of God. And how would we think of Judaism without its tools and reminders of Yahweh, the God of the Jews? What image would this ancient religion present to its adherents without the scriptures of the Torah and Talmud, without synagogues, ceremonies, dietary laws, observances of Rosh Hashanah, Yom Kippur, Passover, Shavuot, Succoth, Hanukkah, and Purim? And as for the vast populations of the Far East who are followers of Buddhism or Hinduism, or one of the offshoots of these religions, what radical changes would there be in the lives of these peoples if the scriptures, temples, shrines, and monasteries were removed together with the special ceremonies, rituals, symbols, and artifacts used in their daily religious routines?

In short, history has clearly shown that religion does not exist without a complex assortment of tools that can focus the attention of the follower upon an abstraction. The abstraction, symbolically kept in sight, is therefore more easily kept in mind.

Can religious symbolism be used to excess? Can the tools of religion be abused and subverted until the original purpose for which they stood is lost or abandoned? Can the means become the end or, as McLuhan might say, can the medium become the message? Indeed, this is an ever present threat. The symbols, themselves, can become the objects of idolatry, displacing the deity which they were chosen to represent. Such was the situation which two reformers, the Buddha Gautama, and Martin Luther, encountered in their day. Each of these men rebelled against what he perceived to be excessive corruption and ritual in his religion. As a result, there emerged from Hinduism the religion of Buddhism, and from Roman Catholicism sprung Protestantism.

The tools of religion have purposes other than those solely and directly concerned with focusing attention on God. The operation of group psychology is an example of such a tool. When numbers of people participate together in a ceremony or ritual, there is found a social interaction and sense of cohesion within the group that tends to give the activity a momentum or life of its own. This herd instinct serves religion as a tool to foster group enthusiasm and fellowship in religious activity. The very nature of religious organization as an interrelated series of activities forms a tool that tends to encourage ongoing involvement once participation has begun. Religion, besides being a human need, is a social habit which, once started, is often easier to continue than to stop. The feeling of common social purpose, when taken together with the buildings, the scriptures, the rituals, and the administrative hierarchy, helps religion achieve a capacity for self regeneration and the unstoppable momentum of a perpetual motion machine. This is not to say, however, that the system is totally resistant to change. Insofar as religion is practiced to satisfy human needs, and because these needs alter as human knowledge expands, so too must religion change.

## DO KNOWLEDGE AND COMPASSION REALLY COUNT?

Like animals, religions evolve. Some become extinct, others persist but adapt. Countless religions have not survived, such as those of Greece, Rome, and Egypt two thousand years ago. These were so-called polytheistic religions with gods of love, war, sun, thunder, wine, water, and many other manifestations of nature. The rare religions that have survived have tended to grow somewhat like a tree. The trunk, or main body, slowly increases in size while giving rise to an increasing number of branches. Thus the Christian religion, established after the death of Jesus, expanded and eventually gave off hundreds of branches represented by the denominations of the Protestant Church today. Similarly, Buddhism, established twenty-five hundred years ago and based on the teachings of a single man, branched after his death into many major divisions and subdivisions. The branching usually arises from a difference of opinion within a religion with regard to the way the doctrine should be interpreted. Thus, we had the separation of Buddhism into the group-oriented (*Mahayana*) and individual-oriented (*Theravada*) schools. Splitting also occurs as a revolt against perceived abuses and corruption within the main trunk. Classic examples of this, as mentioned in the last Section, are the splitting off of Buddhism from the main trunk of Hinduism, and the separation of Luther's Protestant reform movement from the Roman Catholic main stream.

When it comes to alteration of fundamental beliefs and customs within a religion, these usually take place gradually, and reflect new knowledge acquired through advances in science and technology. In the light of current meteorological insight, for example, the worship of a god of rain or thunder would seem silly, whereas it did not to the people of Mesopotamia or Babylon. Similarly, early Egyptian sacrifices to a sun god made more sense at the time than they do today because we know that thermonuclear fusion of atoms powers the sun. Thus, it is quite clear that the advent of new information has modified or eliminated the rational for many former religious beliefs and customs.

Another force that alters religious custom is the emergence and spread of the human attribute of compassion. Compassion slowly seems to be tempering the callous disregard for human suffering shown in former times by both secular and religious authorities. Abuses were not confined to any one religion or state. For example, Islamic doctrine, backed by state authority, specified the cutting off of a man's hand as punishment for stealing, and condoned the stoning to death of adulterers. Hinduism, not to be outdone, approved of widows throwing themselves upon the flames of their husbands' funeral pyres in the ritual of suttee. Cooler heads now prevail in India, and this practice was made illegal earlier in this century. No less macabre were Aztec priests who, as an offering to their gods, sliced out the hearts of sacrificial humans who had been raised and groomed from youth for this special purpose. Incredibly, instances of human killings involving perverse quasi-religious ritual are still perpetrated in today's civilized societies by undercover cults. In the past, the endorsement by, or indifference of, civil authority to the horrendous use of torture and painful execution within religious institutions reached public notoriety particularly through the excesses of the infamous branch offices of the Roman Catholic Church known as the Spanish Inquisition. These fun places operated at a furious pace in many countries during the middle ages. The Inquisition could detain anyone at will simply by alleging that the person might be a heretic and should be questioned. Confessions were routine, and routinely followed by burning. There was no court of appeal except that of the religious administrators themselves. The fox was truly in charge of the hen house.

The various illustrations we have presented showing the absence of compassion in man toward man, rooted in religion with the collusion of the state, are hardly surprising given the rough climate of bygone times where legalized barbarism was often the rule rather than the exception. And these times are not so very distant. For example, slavery, torture, and hanging for petty theft were all alive and well, lawfully administered, and publicly tolerated in many societies only two or three centuries ago. Apparently, the toil that most people had scratching out a living in the stern and unforgiving past, and the need to protect self and family from predatory ruffians of all stripes, often left little scope for compassion. It was perhaps a case of, "I'm just scraping by, Jack, and can't watch out for you." Today's outlook is more encouraging. The legalized use of terror seems to be receding as compassion comes more into vogue.

**THE IMPACT OF RELIGION**

We have looked in this chapter at some of the areas where religion has entered man's life. History and common sense tell us that religion should not be taken lightly. Poor humans, with their compulsion to improve their lot, are constantly questing for answers to those enigmas for which there are no evident answers. Religion has helped us deal with some of these mysteries. It has sanctioned for us a moral code by which to live in harmony. It has helped us cope with distress. Clerics devote whole careers to its pursuit, ascetics abuse themselves in its name, fanatical martyrs are tortured and die for it, entire nations go to war over it. Religion is, well, important. People, whenever and wherever they have lived, from poles to equator, East to West, have been affected personally or indirectly by religion. Surely, it is here at least for the foreseeable future.

Among the major world religions with long histories, five of the best known are: Judaism, Christianity, Hinduism, Buddhism, and Islam. In the next chapter, we will look at some of the things that each of these great religions has to say about God, the soul, and life after death. We should then know if there is any common ground upon which traditional religion might meet with the hypothesis of saved memories as set forth in Chapter 2 of this book.

# THE MAJOR RELIGIONS VERSUS THE SAVED MEMORY HYPOTHESIS

## JUDAISM

*God*: One thing that the five great religions are unanimously agreed upon is the existence of the supernatural. For the Jews, the supernatural is represented by Yahweh, the divine entity or God whom they believe made the universe. 'In the beginning God created the heavens and the earth,' declares Genesis in the first book of the Torah, the earliest Jewish scripture. Since the beginning of the biblical record, the Hebrews believed there was one God only, and He was just, merciful, and loved man. In contrast, the neighboring peoples in Rome, Greece, Syria, Egypt, and Babylonia had many gods, and they were considered by their worshipers to be immoral, vindictive, capricious, and indifferent to man. The God of the early Jews spoke to his people through the biblical prophets, and provided some six hundred and thirteen commandments to be found in the Old Testament exhorting man to be moral, just, and to live in harmony with his fellows. In a Covenant with God, the Jews believe they were chosen to serve and suffer in the redemption of the world in return for God's blessing.

*Life after death*: The books of the Old Testament have very little to say about life after death. Sheol is first mentioned in the 8th Century BC and is described in the Old Testament as the underworld place of departed spirits where there is no hope, no joy, only a shadowy existence without thought of punishment or reward. The Apocalyptic literature which emerged between 200 B. C. and 100 A. D. speaks of paradise and fiery hell, but is considered inconsistent. The subject of reincarnation is not mentioned at all in the Old Testament, although the Talmud, compiled in the early centuries after Christ, contains references to the transmigration of souls, as does the mystical Cabalistic division of Judaism dating from the 2nd Century A. D. Today, belief in an afterlife by the Jewish people ranges from an absolute conviction held by Orthodox Jews to a more moderate hope on the part of Reform Jews.

## CHRISTIANITY

*God*: Christians have the same God as Jews, namely Yahweh of the Old Testament, except that he is divided into three parts. The Christian concept of the Trinity holds that, while God is fully one, He is also three. These are respectively God the Father, God the Son, and God the Holy Spirit. Since Christians, like Jews, consider themselves to be monotheistic, that is, having only one God, this division into three may seem contrary to logic. The paradox is compounded when it is noted that Jesus was regarded as a God-man. The Christian doctrine of the Incarnation holds that God assumed a human body, and affirms that Christ was simultaneously both fully God and fully man. Being two different things at once has also been noted in quantum theory according to which a substance can be simultaneously both a wave and a particle. Christians believe that the Holy Spirit, the third divine component of the Trinity, resides in and animates man's soul, and Roman Catholicism holds that, by a life of prayer, it may disclose its presence to the worshiper and lift him to a state of mystical ecstasy.

*Life after death*: The Christian belief is that, when man dies, his life enters a supernatural domain. If his soul is 'saved', it enters a state of eternal happiness called Heaven. If not saved, the soul may exist eternally in a state of punishment called Hell. The Book of Revelation, written sometime between 81 - 96 AD, says:

'But the fearful, and unbelieving, and the abominable, and murderers, and whoremongers, and sorcerers, and idolaters, and all liars, shall have their part in the lake which burneth with fire and brimstone.' However, this scary scenario has little to do with Christ's teaching and may have been written by a questionable fanatic. There is no consistent model of Hell in the Bible.

Christianity holds that God came to earth in the person of Jesus Christ to teach people how to be saved, pointing out the way they should behave in this world in order to have eternal life in the next. Such beliefs in the immortality of the soul, however, are late additions to Christian thought, and they do not appear anywhere in the Bible. According to Roman Catholic doctrine, the soul may go to Purgatory instead of Heaven or Hell. Purgatory, not mentioned in the New Testament, was an invention of early Christian Fathers who considered it a place or state of temporary punishment, 'where those who have died in the grace of God are expiating their venial faults and such pains as are still due to forgiven mortal sins.' Protestantism rejects the concept of Purgatory. With regard to belief in reincarnation, most Christian theologians today give no credence to the theory. However, as a matter of historical fact, it was accepted up to the time of the Council of Constantinople held in AD 551. Currently, 'New Agers' interpret some references in the Gospels as support for their belief in reincarnation.

## HINDUISM

*Background*: As Eastern and Western cultures are different, so too are their religions. Hinduism, the ancient religion of the East, contrasts with Judaism and its offshoots, the religions that have so strongly influenced the West. Dramatic images of Indian ascetics walking on hot coals or stretched out on beds of nails are perhaps extreme examples that point up differences between the traditional Eastern and Western outlook. The goal to which the seriously religious Hindu aspires is to isolate himself from the physical world, to shut down his senses, to shine the spotlight on his divine interior rather than upon the inconsequential world without. This desire to withdraw from worldly distractions is not shared by the religious Westerner, whose scriptures proclaim: 'God saw everything that He made and behold it was very good.' For the Westerner, physical aspects of existence are to be relished with zest. Genesis proclaims that man should have dominion over all the earth, and such is the Westerner's view. This materialistic appreciation contrasts with the East where there has always been a religiously motivated reluctance to meddle with nature. The common tendency of the Easterner is to leave things as they are, not to interfere with the natural order around him. His liberation lies ultimately in extricating his spirit from its material environment. The Westerner, on the other hand, has an urge to step in when he sees something askew, to straighten it up, make it right, make it better. God made a Covenant with the ancient Hebrews in which he instructed them to go out and create a just society. The social revolutions and scientific advances so prominent in Western history may well stem from this biblical Covenant in which man's God-given role was to improve the world.

*God*: The name the Hindus give to their supreme reality is Brahman. He may be thought of as a personal, compassionate, involved God-with-attributes, *Saguna Brahman*, or as a more abstract God-without-attributes, *Nirguna Brahman*, who stands aloof from earth's struggle. The former, *Saguna Brahman*, who shows love, mercy, power, and understanding, is commonly regarded as existing in three distinct parts, a parallel with the Christian Trinity concept. These three parts are *Brahma*, who created the universe, *Vishnu*, who preserves it, and *Shiva*, who will take it back. The contemporary philosopher and author, Huston Smith, describes Hinduism's blueprint of the universe: 'There would be innumerable galaxies comparable to our own, each focusing in an earth from which men wend their ways to God ... Periodically, the cosmos collapses into a Night of *Brahma*, and all phenomenal being is returned to a state of pure potentiality.

Thus like a gigantic accordion the world swells out and is drawn back in. This oscillation is a permanent feature of existence; the universe had no beginning and will have no end.' This graphic picture conjures up, for the cosmologist, the idea of Big Bangs alternating with Big Crunches without end. In such a world, the Hindu feels that all talk of social progress is to misconstrue God's purpose which is to provide an arena for the training of the soul.

Although Brahman is worshipped as the one God of the Hindu religion, this God is approached, and prayed to, through the medium of hundreds of physical images and artifacts which help to focus and hold the worshiper's mind on an otherwise abstract deity. These symbols of convenience have been described as 'matchmakers, responsible for introducing man' s heart to what they represent but themselves are not.' They are regarded as depicting Brahman in his innumerable aspects. It is therefore not surprising to find Hindus all over the Eastern world worshipping widely divergent symbols of their God. Different Hindu schools also teach that Brahman manifests himself in human form, past examples of which have been Christ, Rama, Krishna, and Buddha.

*Soul*: Hinduism holds that every individual has a separate soul called the *jiva* which is identified with the individual personality. Animating this soul is a divine entity, the *Atman,* which is a part of the supreme God, Brahman. Of this Atman-Brahman concept, Huston Smith has written:

'Underlying man's personality and animating it is a reservoir of being that never dies, is never exhausted, and is without limit in awareness and bliss. This infinite center of every life, this hidden self or *Atman,* is no less than Brahman, the Godhead ... buried under the almost impenetrable mass of distractions, false ideas, and self-regarding impulses that comprise our surface being.'

The Hindu *yogi's* goal is to dig under those surface layers to reveal and become one with the *Atman* that resides deep within him. He will thus accept 'loss and pain with equanimity: such things touch only the surface self whereas his identification is being transferred to the underlying immutable self whose limitless joy and serenity cannot possibly be ruffled by momentary turns of fortune.' This would seem to account for the air of calm and settled peace in the eyes and expression of advanced *yogis*, wandering about in simple rags, alms bowl in hand, without the basic comforts of roof or bed. Through a life of single-minded purpose and the rejection of worldly pleasures, they have been able to discard their egos and achieve an internal bliss that has eluded their physically affluent brothers. This profound ecstasy that is known to the advanced Hindu *yogi*, has its analog, perhaps, in the mystical heights to which a Christian, according to Roman Catholic doctrine, may be transported when the divine soul within him is revealed through a life of constant prayer.

*Life after death*: The Hindu believes that, when he dies, his soul (*jiva*) will depart from his lifeless corpse and enter a newly born body, either that of a human, an animal, or a plant. Note, however, that the soul does not enter the new body immediately, but first must spend a period of time in one of a number of other worlds. Whether the Hindu finds this other world pleasing or not depends on the way he has lived his life on earth prior to death. This idea of rebirth is called reincarnation, and means giving a new physical body to the soul. A long series of such rebirths are thought to occur for each individual until his soul, if all goes well, achieves perfection and is ultimately delivered from the burden of endless reincarnations by the act of being absorbed into the substance of the universal God, Brahman. After this absorption, the individual's soul will never again be reborn as a separate entity, but will remain in eternal, blissful union with Brahman. The concept of reincarnation or transmigration of souls will be explored further in the next chapter.

## BUDDHISM

*Background*: Buddhism grew out of the Hindu religion, and retains much of the Hindu philosophy which existed long before this new sect emerged as a reaction against the ritualistic, corrupted state of Hinduism in India twenty-five hundred years ago. These two great religions of Indian origin, Buddhism and Hinduism, share a common outlook on life. For example, the serious Buddhist monk and the dedicated Hindu *yogi* would both probably tell us that the closeness to which they can approach their religious goals depends on the degree to which they are able to detach their minds from the distractions of the non-real physical world and concentrate upon what is significant, namely, the reality of the inner being. Buddhism and Hinduism do not differ much with respect to this basic belief. However, unlike the Hindu, the Buddhist believes in no personal God, Brahman. Neither does the Buddhist think that he has an individual, immortal soul (Jiva/Atman), nor is his conception of reincarnation the same as that of the Hindu. Finally, another difference may be noted: that Buddhism was founded by one individual, Siddhartha Gautama, born in northern India about 560 BC, whereas the roots of Hinduism are far more diffuse and spring from no such single source.

*God*: What did the Buddha, Gautama, have to say about God? Not much. One of the few references that he made to a supernatural being has been quoted: 'There is, O monks, an Unborn, neither become nor created nor formed ... Were there not, there would be no deliverance from the born, the made, the compounded.' This is perhaps as close as Gautama, in the vast Pali scriptures, comes to a concept of God.

It has been truthfully stated that the Buddha's religion was psychological rather than metaphysical. Gautama dealt with man's problems in the here and now, and was reluctant to be drawn into any discussion of creation, God, the specifics of an afterlife, or metaphysical concepts. Instead of speculating with regard to cosmic creation and then focusing on man's role in it, Gautama concentrated from the beginning upon man, his challenges, his essence, his growth, and resisted discussion of any larger metaphysical picture. However, the state of Nirvana, the enlightened mental condition to which every serious Buddhist aspires, has been described as close enough to the idea of God that it may be thought of as similar to a Godhead. Nevertheless, Gautama specifically denied the existence of the gods of Hinduism and of other religions. It is interesting to note that, in violation of his own philosophy, Gautama himself came to be deified within some sects of Buddhism after his death.

*Soul*: What did the Buddha have to say about the soul? In his teaching, Gautama said that man has no soul in the sense that soul means a spiritual substance that holds its distinct nature eternally. He thus did not agree with the Hindu's idea of an individual *Atman*, or divine soul, which is destined ultimately to be reunited with Brahman, or God. The concept of a changeless *Atman*, one that has no beginning or end, which forms the basic essence of each of us, clearly contrasts with Gautama's *anatta*, or no soul, doctrine.

*Life after death*: When the Buddha, Gautama, was asked what happens after bodily death to the individual who, in life, has attained to Nirvana, his replies were mysterious and subject to different interpretations. The nearest we can come to a consensus regarding his meaning is that the final destiny of the human spirit is a condition in which all identification with the finite, earthly self and its memories will disappear, while experience itself will remain and find itself augmented beyond human capacity to imagine. Apart from Gautama's reticence in answering metaphysical questions, the fact that several centuries elapsed after his death before his remembered words were set down in literary form must surely have scrambled to some unknown degree the accuracy and precision of his recorded views on spirit life. One of the Buddha's disciples is reported to have said:

'Whether the world is eternal or not eternal, whether the world is finite or not, whether the soul is the same as the body or whether the soul is one thing and the body another, whether a Buddha exists after death or does not exist after death — these things the Lord (Gautama) does not explain to me.'

"The one thing I teach," said Buddha, "is suffering and the end of suffering." Thus Gautama would discourage his disciples from indulging in the agreeable but profitless field of metaphysical speculation which he believed would only divert them from the pragmatic eight-fold path to Nirvana. The literal meaning of Nirvana is extinction, but the Buddhist uses the word to mean extinction of the ego or finite self, not the extinction of being. Gautama said that Nirvana is "incomprehensible, indescribable, inconceivable, unutterable ... bliss."

After Gautama's death, his followers ultimately split into two main groups with regard to the way his teachings should be interpreted. The first group (Theravada or Hinayana) employed a rather strict, literal interpretation. The second group (Mahayana) was far more flexible.

Today, within the group of Theravada Buddhists, Nirvana is thought about in one of two ways, according to John Hick, a contemporary student of religion:

1. as a psychological state in a living person such that, when the person dies, he and his state of Nirvana "simply pass out of existence ... and are no more;"

2. as an immortal, spiritual reality. At death, the individual who in life attained to Nirvana merges with, or becomes one with, this reality. Whether or not he retains some sense of his separate individuality is open to interpretation.

When Buddhism split into the Theravada and Mahayana schools, as noted above, the Mahayana division, which was the more liberal and popular of the two, 'spawned an elaborate cosmology' according to the contemporary philosopher Huston Smith, 'replete with innumerable heavens, hells, and descriptions of Nirvana ... (with Buddha) who was an atheist in respect to belief in a personal God transmogrified into such a God himself ... come to earth to draw men into the ultimate reality.' According to Mahayana doctrine, death releases the spirit to wander for up to one hundred days in a Bardo state after which rebirth takes place. The Mahayanist Bardo Thodol ('The Tibetan Book of the Dead'), which was written about the eighth century A. D., outlines the sequence of experiences undergone by the 'conscious mind' during the forty-nine days between death and its reincarnation in a new body. These experiences are considered to be projections of the mind of the deceased, and involve images of loved ones, awareness of various forms of light, and assorted nightmare-like apparitions of a thoroughly scary nature.

With regard to reincarnation, the Buddhist doctrine, as conceived by Gautama, seems more vague and contradictory than that of the Hindus. Gautama denied the Hindu notion of a soul which passes from one body to another, but accepted the Hindu concept of *karma* which holds that the deeds of one life are instrumental in the shaping of the subsequent life. Although Buddhism asserts that there is no self, or historical memory link, that remains intact through any series of rebirths, we are faced with the paradox that Gautama himself, and other enlightened *Arhats* that succeeded him, claim to remember the events of thousands of their past lives. The 'logical' Western mind groans and boggles when it tries to grasp and reconcile these seemingly illogical and irreconcilable contradictions.

## ISLAM

*Background*: Islam! The very word conjures up images in the minds of some Westerners of fanatical, unruly mobs, religious ruffians, a rude, inscrutable culture practicing cruel, primitive justice. This may, indeed, have been the case in Mecca before the 6th Century A. D. and also in many other places of the world at that time, but the birth of Mohammed, the founder of Islam, about 571 A. D. changed Arab society enormously for the better through his preaching of rigorous moral behavior and orderly conduct.

It is seldom recognized by Westerners that Islam and Christianity share a lot in common. For example, both have their roots in the religion of the Jews, Judaism, and both point to the biblical figure of Abraham as their common ancestor. Muslims and Christians, alike, hold sacred the ten commandments handed down to Moses as a model for human conduct, and both religions advocate a moral code of love and justice which is written in their scriptures, the Koran and the Bible.

What is it that sets these great religions, Islam and Christianity, apart, that makes the devout Muslim and the serious Christian different in their religious conduct? The main difference, perhaps, involves the much stricter code of behavior that is required of the Muslim by the Koran. This word of God, delivered to the Prophet Mohammed and written down by Mohammed's followers, did not leave to chance or philosophical debate how each and every Muslim was to pray, dress, eat, and live. God spelled it all out, dotting the i's and crossing the t's. The Koran states exactly what each Muslim must, and must not, do in order to live a righteous life and attain Paradise. The Christian Bible, on the contrary, is more flexible. It gives wider license to individual discretion with regard to the manner in which God's wishes are to be fulfilled. How many wives may a man take? Jesus didn't say, but Mohammed mentioned four. How should the poor be treated? The Bible says generously, but the Koran specifies two and a half percent of a man's wealth annually. How often should one pray to God? Frequently, advocated Christ, whereas Mohammed was more precise, stipulating five times a day, at certain periods of the day, and in a specific way facing Mecca.

*God*: The devout Muslim cries out over the rooftops loud and clear for all the world to hear: "There is no God but Allah, and Mohammed is his Prophet." Well, what about the God of the Christians? Is the Christian deity the same God that the Muslim is proclaiming? This tricky question has long been debatable. The Christian worshiper will argue that he, too, is monotheistic and worships only one God, the God of Abraham and Moses, the Yahweh of Judaism. "Ah, but," counters the Muslim, "that God happens to be our God, Allah." "Maybe so," replies the Christian, "but it has been revealed to us that He is really composed of three parts, a Trinity. And by the way, one of those three parts is Jesus, the Son of God." "Nonsense," says the Muslim with the conviction of one who knows the real truth. "Allah has no Son! Allah is the supreme and only divinity, the almighty Creator, undivided, one. Jesus was an important Prophet like Mohammed, but definitely not divine. There is no God but Allah." And so the controversy goes.

*Soul*: When the devout Muslim thinks about the soul, the image that comes to his mind is similar to that which comes to the mind of his Christian cousin. The human soul, says Islam, was created by an act of God's will, and represents God's supreme accomplishment. It is the essence of man's being, and once created, the individual soul is eternal. Both the Koran and the Bible disclose a high regard for the soul as an expression of man's individuality. This contrasts with the scriptures of Eastern religions which downplay the importance of man's individual personality or separateness, regarding the personality, in fact, as an impediment to man's ultimate awareness of reality.

*Life after death*: The Koran teaches that, on the day of Judgment after death, each individual will be accountable for the way he has lived. There is a narrow bridge which crosses over hell to paradise. If the dead candidate has led a wicked life and is judged wanting, he will fall off the bridge into hell and everlasting torment. If he is, on the other hand, judged worthy, he will reach paradise and, according to Mohammed, '... see his Lord's face night and morning ... .' This concept of man's destiny is not unlike that of the Roman Catholic Christian who, according to Maurice and Louis Becque, at the moment of death when the soul separates from the body, is accorded a judgment that is marked by two qualities: 'it is irrevocable and it is immediate ... heaven, purgatory, or hell.'

What is heaven? According to the Koran, it abounds in deep rivers of cool, crystal water, lush fruit and vegetables, boundless fertility, and beautiful mansions with gracious attendants. One can imagine that these images of water and green growth would be especially attractive to the Arab used to scuffling for basic sustenance in the dry, barren desert. We hear about religious Muslims willingly sacrificing themselves in car bombs or minefields for such instant rewards in heaven. However, if the Muslim has any doubts about his ability to cross the bridge to paradise, he may wish to think twice about contracting for a premature passage to hell which Islam describes for him as a scalding crater of molten metal, boiling liquids, and fire. These images would be particularly repellent to the Arab, perhaps, who spends a lifetime battling the heat of sun and sand. With regard to this vivid imagery of heaven and hell, it is written in the Koran that some of the signs are firm, some are figurative.

Does the Muslim believe in Purgatory? Yes, the Koran speaks of a kind of intermediary place situated between the pleasures of paradise and the torments of hell where those who were neither good nor wicked will go. The Roman Catholic concept of Purgatory, by comparison, is a state where the guilty actions of a man's life may be completely effaced after death. Does the Muslim believe, like the Hindu, in the reincarnation of the soul in a series of innumerable rebirths on earth? No. Like Christians, the vast majority of Muslims reject such theories. Neither do the Muslims, unlike the Christians, accept the concept that God was incarnated on earth in the form of Jesus Christ. They accept the historical fact of Jesus as a man and a prophet of God, but consider it naive to suppose that he was God made into flesh.

## HOW DOES THE HYPOTHESIS OF SAVED MEMORIES FIT WITH THE MAJOR RELIGIONS?

Maybe we can have ourselves a little fun at this point by seeing how our 'saved memories' hypothesis relates to ideas that have been incorporated into thousands of years of religious history. To assist the reader's recall, it might be helpful to briefly summarize the main elements of the saved memories hypothesis as follows:

1. Our living Self is compounded from three basic elements: *sensory input*, which is sent to the *memory*, which is accessed by *consciousness*.

2. During life, as memory data are stored in the brain, they are also continuously translocated to another storage medium in another set of dimensions (God leaning on the save button).

3. At some time after death, the translocated memory is ac-

cessed again by consciousness, reconstituting awareness of past life.

4. A quantum physical world of expanded dimensions coexisting with our known universe provides the milieu for events 2 and 3.

How do these ideas correspond to, or contradict, current religious thought? Do they go with the flow, or against it? Our hypothesis has neither the burning faith of religion for support, nor is it confirmed by scientific observation. We only have a guess which may, or may not, be testable. Nevertheless, this guess is an educated one, based on empirical observations of what appears possible. Like any unproved set of assumptions, including those of religion, the saved memory hypothesis is only speculation until verified in whole or in part. Speculation, however, is the frequent precursor of discovery.

*Contrasting views on materialism*: For the Western religions of Judaism, Christianity, and Islam, materialism is important. After all, according to Genesis, in the beginning God created the heavens and the earth. God saw everything that He made, and behold it was very good. Further, God said that man should have dominion over all the earth. In other words, the physical, material world is something made by God and it has value. Man should relish it with zest and use it to his advantage. The Eastern religions, on the other hand, do not share this materialistic appreciation. For Buddhists and Hindus, liberation is equivalent to extricating the spirit from its material environment by ignoring whatever pain or pleasure may be present in the physical world.

Now, where does our concept of transposed memories stand with respect to these contrasting religious ideas? The answer is: it seems to fit with either approach equally well. The hypothesis proposes that the continuity of self awareness beyond death must be associated with the memory of past life. Whether this memory focuses upon the recall of one's relation to the material world, or upon the recall of an introspective state of mind, would seem to have no bearing on the potential for the translocation of that memory. To the extent that post mortem memory remains intact and is accessed, the saved memories concept alleges that self awareness will continue.

*God as power and purpose*: We, as humans, like to think that every effect has a cause. Therefore, when we speculate about memories being transposed from the brain to another set of dimensions, we ask ourselves: how could this occur? By what means, miracle, or magic could such a mysterious achievement be brought about? What cause could produce such an effect? Can we invoke the power of God?

Of course we can. The reader may have noted in the last chapter that ancient man, when puzzled or alarmed by some event that he could not explain, resolved his dilemma by concluding that whatever had happened, whether earthquake, thunder, or tidal wave, was due to the direct intervention of a god. Similarly, when modern man, steeped in science, asks himself how he and the world got here, and where the laws come from that run the universe, the answers elude him, so he deals with the problem the same way that his ancestors did: by invoking the power of God as the agent of cause.

When it comes to the transposition of memories, we are unable at present to point to any known mechanism that would account for such a phenomenon. So, what do we do? Do we throw the hypothesis out because it doesn't, for the moment, appear to be testable? No. Instead, we speculate that God is fully able to make this transposition happen even though our scientists are not yet conversant with His methods. As science gathers more information, it is not unreasonable to expect that the hypothesis of saved memories may lend itself to testing, and thereby be proved, disproved, or modified. If the hypothesis were proved valid, scientists would be unlikely to rest until the details were fully worked out.

Now, if God does indeed transpose memories, which God is responsible? Is it Allah, the one God of Islam? Is it the Christian Trinity of the Father, the Son, and the Holy Ghost? Or Yahweh, the one God of the Hebrews? Or Hinduism's Brahman (with or without "attributes")? Or even the "Unborn" referred to by the Buddha, Siddhartha Gautama? Whichever God is invoked, He would have to be exercising great power, and perhaps purpose.

As far as power is concerned, we don't appear to have a problem, for whichever God was responsible for creating this incredibly wonderful and complex universe, He obviously has power to spare. Anything that could be conjured up in the human imagination would be presumably do-able by God. The feat of transferring and reactivating memories might be, for Him, a mere 'bagatelle' less imposing even than designing and constructing a human brain, or inventing the multidimensional parameters of quantum physics. It might be said, then, that the hypothesis of saved memories is not only compatible with God, but *requires* Him.

If we move now from God's power to His purpose, the picture is less clear. Notwithstanding Einstein's famous remark about God not playing dice with the universe, there is no way to demonstrate whether or not the universe is guided by a purpose or plan. Intuitively we feel that it is, otherwise it would be chaotic or not exist at all. If purpose is indeed instrumental in the modeling of the universe, we would logically assume that the same purpose also extends to us and our self awareness. Prolonging self awareness after death would presumably allow for its further development and enrichment, and so may simply constitute a case of getting on with the unfinished business of man's destiny. In this sense, the reconstituted memory hypothesis may be compared to the ideas of both Eastern and Western religions where further maturation of the soul after death is envisioned by reincarnation or in a supernatural domain.

*Contrasting views of the soul*: Suppose you ask somebody: "What is the soul?" The answer you get would probably depend on that person's religion. You could expect the Theravadan Buddhist to answer: "There is no such thing as a soul." To him, the notion of an immutable identity (*atman*) without beginning or end in each of us is explicitly rejected by Buddha's *anatta* (no soul) doctrine.

Now, a Hindu *yogi,* if he overheard such a question and answer, would likely smile wryly and shake his head in gentle disapproval. Traditional Hindu thought regards individual human souls (*jivas*) as having existed through unlimited time. Sooner or later the soul (*jiva*), after countless reincarnations, is united with God (*atman*) existing deep within the body, and the *Jiva/atman* is delivered from the cycle of rebirths by absorption into Brahman, the Godhead.

Let us suppose that, as our Hindu wanders off seeking alms, we approach a Christian and a Muslim who, by chance, are strolling together, and we ask them: "What is the soul?" Either one might reply to this effect: "The soul is the essence of the human being, created by God, destined to be immortal. If the individual has led a moral life, the soul, with a new spiritual body, ultimately enters a state of eternal happiness in the presence of God. If the individual, instead, has committed evil deeds and not repented, the soul may spend eternity in a state of punishment." Neither the Christian nor the Muslim has anything to say about multiple reincarnations of the soul on earth.

Finally, let us suppose that we encounter a pedestrian who clutches a copy of this very book, *Surviving Death,* in his hand. We assume from this that he may be an advocate of the Saved Memory Hypothesis, and we ask him: "What is the soul?" He glances at the Christian and Muslim still loitering nearby, clears his throat, and replies: "If by 'soul' you refer to the Self, that is, the sense of self awareness that every individual has, then the soul is what survives the death of the body. In its new multidimensional environment, the soul may acquire a new body adapted to interact with its new environment. One can further speculate that the soul could find itself in community with other post mortem 'souls' quite able to continue the soul growth which was begun on earth and which makes of it an increasingly complex entity." Having delivered himself of these pearls, the advocate of saved memories moves off in search of the author of his book desiring to get it autographed.

When we stand and ponder these various viewpoints, we can

find no universal consensus. The Buddhist says, no soul, period. The Hindu says yes, there is a soul perfected through multiple rebirths on earth and then merged in bliss with the eternal Brahman. Wrong, say the Christian and Muslim, there are no rebirths because the soul, if it eludes Satan, rises to the eternal joy of a supernatural domain where, before God, it is further perfected. The saved memories advocate hedges. He will only say that there are rational grounds to believe that the Self could survive death and continue to develop in a new milieu. The delicate thread of agreement that is shared by the Hindu, Christian, Muslim, and saved memories advocate relates to the existence of a soul, its immortality, and its ongoing evolution. The Buddhist does not concur with any of these concepts.

*Anticipating death*: Although we all anticipate that we will die sooner or later, is there any reason to dwell on the prospect? We live in the present, the here and now, so what good does it do to morbidly reflect on death? When its over, its over, the fat lady sings, and that's that. What is due to happen will happen, and there is little we can do about it. Right?

Wrong, says religion. The here and now is less than a drop of water in the Pacific Ocean, less than a grain of sand in the Sahara Desert. By contrast, Eternity is forever, a timeless existence that lies before us. The bottom line is this: what we do in this life, according to most religious thinkers, will determine the way we spend the infinite eternity that awaits us after we die. Let's take a closer look at this idea and its obvious importance, if true, for each one of us. Let's compare some different viewpoints on life after death.

You will remember that, a few paragraphs back, we imagined asking a Buddhist, a Christian, a Muslim, and an advocate of saved memories, what they thought about the soul. Suppose now that the Christian to whom we spoke is standing across the street leafing through a copy of the New Testament.

We go up to him and ask: "What happens to us when we die?"

The Christian does not hesitate: "We go," he answers, "to Heaven, Purgatory, or Hell. Catholics go to Purgatory, some of them, but it is only temporary. If you believe in Christ and keep the Sacraments, its directly to Heaven, for sure."

The Muslim, fingering his Koran, has overheard the conversation, and joins the group. "It's true what the Christian says," he declares, "except the part about the Sacraments and Christ. Jesus was not a God. There is only one God, Allah."

The Hindu, who has had no luck with his alms bowl, now approaches and quietly intones: "There are many other higher and lower realms or planes of existence in which souls can live between reincarnations. In these heavenly, purgatorial, or hellish spheres, the soul reaps the consequences of good or evil deeds done in this world." He pauses to smile indulgently. "But, gentlemen, it is only in the physical body, on earth, that the soul is able to undergo further stages of development toward the ultimate self awareness that we call *moksha*."

"You are mistaken there," says the Christian. "Irenaean theology clearly states that the soul-making process extends beyond this earthly scene to other supernatural worlds."

"Well, I disagree with that," rejoins the Hindu. "And by the way, there is no permanent hell and no eternal damnation."

The Muslim jumps in: "That is where you are wrong, sir. Check your Koran."

A passing Orthodox Jew, who has picked up on some of the remarks, stops long enough to thumb rapidly through the Torah. He announces: "There is nothing in here specifically about Heaven or Hell. When you die, gentlemen, you go to Sheol. That is a shadowy sort of place, no fun, a rotten experience. I hope I don't go."

The others remain silent, so the Jew turns on his heel and leaves. The Christian speaks to the Muslim: "Never mind about the rabbi. I agree with this Hindu chap about further stages of soul development. But reincarnation is nonsense. The development occurs in Heaven. Remember, Jesus said, 'In the house of the Father, there are many Mansions.'"

He turns to direct a meaningful glance at the Hindu, but that frustrated *yogi*, seeing a prospect for alms, has left. A clock is heard striking noon, and the Muslim drops to his prayer rug. The Christian, left alone, decides to say a few Hail Marys, then departs.

Now, what might the saved memories advocate have contributed to this verbal interchange if he had been present? Would he have had any relevant views? Let' s imagine that the Christian, Muslim, Hindu and Jew have met once more, and are being addressed by the advocate of saved memories.

**Advocate**: "Gentlemen, your ideas on death and the hereafter are interesting, but fanciful. The book which I hold here in my hand, *Surviving Death*, is more realistic, I submit, than your scriptures. It deals with how we get from here to there. Unfortunately, it is not yet autographed."

**Jew**: "What does it say, already?"

**Advocate**: "It postulates that all memories are saved. You can get the details from Chapter 2, so I won't bother you with them here. The bottom line is this: there are three important elements in any transition to a post mortem world. They are memories, memories, memories." The Advocate looks from face to face to measure the effect of his words.

**Muslim**: "There is only one God, Allah, and His prophet is Mohammed!"

**Advocate**: "Maybe so, sir, but let me ask you this. Have you ever heard of the expression 'You can't take it with you'? Well, it's wrong! You can jolly well take your memories with you."

**Christian**: "Says who?"

**Advocate**: "The hypothesis of saved memories. It's in this book."

**Christian**: "What's so damned ... I mean, what's so confounded important about memories?"

**Muslim**: "There is only one God ... ."

**Advocate**: "I'm glad you asked that question about memories. Memories, you see, are the only thing you take with you when you die. They make you accountable. If the memories are evil, you carry your own hell as baggage. If they are good, you have created your own heaven."

**Christian**: "Nonsense. When, and if, you get to Heaven, you will have a new existence in the presence of God."

**Advocate**: "Possibly, but .... ."

**Muslim**: "There is only one God, Allah, and... ."

**Advocate:** "... possibly, I say ... but, regardless, you will relive your memories in exquisite detail, over and over, like the reincarnations of our Hindu friend here."

The Hindu, who has been rocking gently on the balls of his bare feet while making snoring noises, opens an eye and leers.

**Hindu**: "What *yogi* says your book is right?"

**Advocate**: "No *yogi*, nobody. But the hypothesis in this book, of which I am trying to locate the author, is obviously extrapolated from fact, not fancy."

**Jew**: "Sounds off the wall to me."

**Advocate**: "No, sir. Even your shadowy Sheol could be a garbled replay of some bad memories. Remember, our memories outlive death."

**Jew**: "Where... at what place are these so-called dead memories located? They must exist somewhere, certainly not in the dead person's head?"

The Hindu, who has been meditating upon reincarnation, is now wide awake, and speaks with missionary zeal.

**Hindu**: "On earth, it takes place! Rebirth happens on Earth. The soul is transferred into a newborn body of flesh."

The Jew peers at the Hindu, then turns to the Advocate.

**Jew**: "Do you buy that?"

**Advocate**: "Well, no. This Hindu chap relies on the doctrine of reincarnation to back up his idea of karma. He thinks that past wrongs are ultimately made right through a series of consecutive rebirths on earth. No, I don't buy that, nor do I believe in the tooth fairy."

**Christian**: "Do you believe that the soul reaches perfection through stages? And if so, where does this take place?"

**Advocate**: " What you call the soul, I prefer to think of as self awareness. Self awareness is a changing thing, in life and probably after life. As to where these changes may take place following death of the body, the hypothesis in this book suggests a possible milieu; namely, the dimensions of quantum physics. We have a glimmer of evidence that these dimensions exist, that they are multiple, that they are unusual, and mysterious. We are not dealing here with a supernatural, never-never land of the imagination. The quantum world is quite real with measurable parameters."

**Jew**: "Thin evidence to build a theory on."

**Advocate**: "Saved memories is no theory, only a hypothesis; pure speculation, until tested."

**Muslim**: "It is not in the Koran."

**Jew**: "Nor in the Torah."

**Hindu**: "It's not written in the Upanishads, nor have I seen it in the Bhagavad Gita."

**Christian**: "Well, it's certainly not in the Bible."

The Advocate of saved memories prepares to leave, book in hand, saying:

**Advocate**: "Gentlemen, the ideas that I share with you today have neither been verified, nor falsified. The case for saved memories rests on rational assumptions, I can say no more. You might want to get hold of a copy of this book."

The motley group, looking skeptical to a man, disperses while wondering if it would be an act of heresy to read such a volume. The Advocate, for his part, has heard that the author may be found quaffing ale at a local watering hole around the corner, and repairs thence post haste for a possible autograph.

## ANYTHING IS POSSIBLE

To analyze man's belief in the supernatural is not to condemn it. It should be emphasized that, although there is no evidence *for* a continuance of life in this, or in a parallel world, neither is there any evidence *against* it. The question is open. It would be foolish to discredit religious doctrine and belief in an afterlife simply because we have no hard data to support it. There is every reason to suspect that many phenomena may occur in our environment about which we are completely ignorant. A blind man cannot detect the presence of the moon or the stars, nor can a deaf man hear a bird sing or the sound of waves breaking on the shore. Our senses and our instruments may be woefully remiss in covering all bases. This potential for the existence of undetected phenomena has enabled every sort of speculation to flourish not only in ancient times but also alongside modern science. As science advances, however, we will have more and more opportunity to find out which beliefs are warranted and which are not.

# REINCARNATION

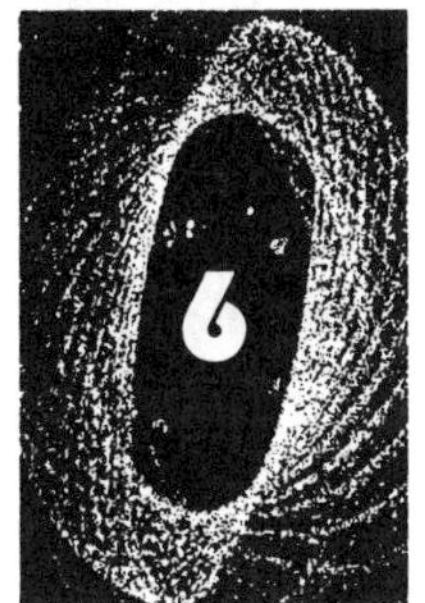

When this book was in the planning stage, an outline was sent to various literary agents who act as go-betweens for author and publisher. One of these agents, an American, wrote back that he was not the right person to represent the book because, as his letter said,

'For me, reincarnation is plausible and far more exciting than what science would have us believe. Birth and rebirth makes sense to me in an evolutionary context: we are here to learn valuable lessons from one lifetime to the next. It feels right and I like the magic of that, your learned explanation notwithstanding.'

The agent felt he was the wrong person to market a book that did not unreservedly embrace the doctrine of reincarnation. I respect this uncompromising idealism, but the attitude raises certain questions. Why this strong reaction from a Westerner? The doctrine of reincarnation is usually identified with the religions of Hinduism, Buddhism, and Jainism of the far East, not with Christianity, Judaism, and Islam of the West. What causes this American literary agent, together with millions of other Western occidentals, to choose the Eastern concept of mankind's destiny rather than that of the West? Why a belief in a cycle of multiple rebirths on earth rather than a direct passage to Heaven, or even oblivion, when life leaves the body? If it is the evolution of the soul toward perfection that we are concerned with, why should we believe that this could proceed any more effectively by the process of reincarnation in this world rather than in Heaven in the presence of God or, for that matter, in the theoretical quantum domain postulated by the Saved Memory Hypothesis set forth in Chapter 2 of this book? What, in fact, does the doctrine of reincarnation have to say that has captured the interest of so many people in this world? What attraction does it hold that is today causing so many Westerners to convert from their orthodox beliefs to the 'magic', as the literary agent calls it, of the idea of reincarnation? What is the credibility of reincarnation in the light of objective analysis?

For people who like to base their opinions on hard evidence received through their 5 senses, the credibility is slight. To others, who are less rigid in their thinking, and perhaps more inclined toward an intuitive interpretation of nature, the credibility is impressive. Thus, about half the world believes in some form of reincarnation. This includes the Hindus and Buddhists of such countries as India, China, Japan, Thailand, Burma, Sri Lanka, Cambodia, Mongolia, Tibet and Korea. As we saw from the literary agent's letter, even Westerners, and this applies especially to the group known as 'New Agers', are becoming more and more intrigued today with the idea of multiple rebirths on earth. However, just because half the world believes in it does not make it so. For example, at one time a majority of the world's inhabitants thought the earth was flat, and they were wrong. Again, most people once assumed that the sun circled a stationary earth. Again, they were wrong. Careful research and discovery have cleared up a multitude of mistaken impressions concerning the ways and workings of nature, continually adding accuracy and definition to our interpretation of the universe. What have research and discovery yielded with regard to the concept of reincarnation? Let's take a look at the reincarnation hypothesis, and briefly comment on at least one investigative attempt to verify it.

## WHAT IS THE REINCARNATION HYPOTHESIS?

Literally, the word 'incarnate' means 'in the flesh'. Reincarnation denotes something put in the flesh again, that is, given a new body. Actually, in the common usage of the word, reincarnation does not refer to flesh only, for the new body may be a tree, a stone, anything. And what is this 'something' which gets a new body and loses an old one? The 'something' is what the Hindus call the soul, an eternal spiritual substance which can change bodies. They say that the soul leaves the old body at death, and passes into another newly born one. This process of jumping from one body to another, like an agile flea, can be repeated thousands — some say an endless number — of times.

The word reincarnation is more or less interchangeable with other terms by which the concept of rebirth is also known, such as transmigration, metempsychosis, and palingenesis. They all refer to the passage of the soul through a sequence of bodies. Early in this sequence, before the soul acquires a human body, it is said to pass through a series of non-human bodies, each one more complex than the last, until finally as a crowning achievement it obtains a human form. Up to this point, the soul's growth is considered to be virtually *automatic*. Now, in a human body, the soul reaches self consciousness for the first time, and with this comes freedom and responsibility where every decision must have its determinate consequence. The career of a soul as it threads its course through innumerable human bodies is guided by its moral choices until, if and when perfection is reached, it passes into identification with God and escapes the otherwise endless, burdensome cycle of rebirths.

Thus, there is a purpose, or rational, ascribed to this onerous series of rebirths which is associated with what the Hindus call *karma*. *Karma* refers to an individual's deeds and thoughts during life, and it is these deeds and thoughts which determine what kind of body, and what quality of existence, will be enjoyed or suffered in the next life. 'You make your bed and you sleep in it,' or 'as a man sows, so shall he reap'. *Karma* is the principle according to which the soul is being continually judged and educated. It is the moral law of cause and effect. The consequences of man's past decisions condition his present lot, and his present decisions determine his future states. In this way, each individual gets exactly what he deserves. And reincarnation is the means by which this purpose is realized. Or so it is thought by something like half the human population of this planet.

## DIALOGUE BETWEEN A YOGI AND A LEMONADE MAN

The Hindu *yogi* who, in the last chapter, was talking to a Christian, a Jew, a Muslim, and an Advocate of Saved Memories, decides to leave town with his alms bowl in order to try his luck in the next village. We find him footsore and thirsty, trudging a dusty trail under an unbelievably hot sun. It is past noon, and he has not tasted water since dawn. The pain from his blistered feet makes it difficult to keep his thoughts on a spiritual plane.

Presently, squinting into the steamy distance, the *yogi* is surprised to spy a truck parked in the shade of some palms. As he gets closer, he can see a sign that reads 'Lemonade Sold Here', and is able to make out a colorful awning, table, chairs, and a young man busy with bins of ice and vats of water. When the Hindu is within hailing distance, the young stranger speaks to him in English:

"Would you like to stop and rest, Sir? Have a drink of ice cold lemonade?"

The *yogi* stands staring until the young man addresses him again.

"Please sit." He points to a chair. "You'll be comfortable here in the shade. Will you have the medium, or jumbo size lemonade?"

"I have no money," croaked the *yogi*.

The lemonade vendor's eye took in the traveler's sorry rags, his empty bowl, his dripping brow.

"That's okay," he said. "It's on the house." He lifted a big white jug, dew drops glistening on its surface, and poured lemonade and crushed ice into a jumbo cup. "There you go," he grinned, holding out the brimming cup.

"But I can't pay," insisted the *yogi*.

"I said it's on the house."

"Bless you, Sir." The *yogi* gulped the cold greenish liquid, and it was soon gone.

"I suppose you are a religious man?" queried the vendor, ogling the ascetic looking Indian.

"I am a *yogi*, and grateful for your lemonade," avowed the Hindu, darting sideways glances at the jug.

"Thought you might be a *yogi*," mused the vendor. "I'm a theology student."

The *yogi's* cracked lips managed a smile. "Your accent is American."

"Uhuh. Baltimore. Know it?"

"A Baltimore man dispensing lemonade in Bombay." The Indian wrinkled his brow, letting a bead of sweat fall into an eye.

The young vendor grinned. "Well, just rounding out my education." He watched the *yogi* wipe out the sweat. "Come to think of it....maybe we could help each other." Another lemonade was poured.

"In what way may I help you, my friend?" asked the Hindu.

"You could tell me about reincarnation. I've got a college assignment due on it. You talk, I'll keep the juice flowing." He handed the brimming cup to the parched Indian.

"Thank you, Sir, you are very kind, your lemonade is excellent. What would you like to know?"

The vendor guided his wizened companion to a chair, and pointed to the jug.

"Help yourself."

The *yogi* complied and, suitably refreshed, entered into the following dialogue with the lemonade man.

**YOGI**: "Now, what is it you wish to know about the cycle of rebirth?"

**VENDOR**: "Do *you* think it happens?"

**YOGI**: "Yes. It happens."

**VENDOR**: "How do you know?"

**YOGI**: "Well, the soul has to be perfected. Every soul has lessons to learn. It can't be done in one lifetime."

He held up a single finger and shook his head. "Do you see, each reincarnation gives the soul a chance for further development, further betterment."

**VENDOR**: "What's the evidence?"

**YOGI**: "How else can the soul reach perfection and be absorbed into Brahman?"

**VENDOR**: "That's not evidence. That's speculation."

**YOGI**: "What do you mean by evidence?" The Hindu swirled the slush in the bottom of his cup.

**VENDOR**: "Hard evidence. I know you're here in front of me because I can see you, hear you, smell you." He wrinkled his nose and grinned in mock distaste.

The Hindu remained silent for a moment, refilled his cup, and looked at the young student with appraising eyes.

**YOGI**: "Are you familiar, Sir, with the work of Dr. Ian Stevenson?"

**VENDOR:** "Yeah. He's into reincarnation in a big way. Interviewed hundreds of kids about their supposed past lives."

**YOGI**: "Dr. Stevenson's work is the most solid evidence we have, of the type I think you would call objective. Do you know that he has over two thousand case histories in his files ... of children who remember at least one past life in another body?"

The American smiled at the Hindu, and nodded approvingly.

**VENDOR:** "I see you're up on your psychical research, Mr. *Yogi*. Are you familiar with the criticisms of Stevenson' s work? The problems?"

**YOGI**: "There are some."

**VENDOR:** "Let me list a few. Most of the kids that have been interviewed don't speak English, so the interviewers use interpreters. This can color what's said. The interviewers get to the scene maybe years after the memories are first reported. This means the stories get changed. And the kids are all tuned in to the reincarnation idea ... it's part of their culture. All this is not very objective, Mr. *Yogi*."

**YOGI**: "Conditions cannot always be perfect, can they?"

**VENDOR:** "Has Stevenson's work been checked by any other researchers?"

**YOGI**: "Not to my knowledge. It will be. And methods will improve."

**VENDOR**: "This is hardly evidence, Sir. This is anecdotal hear-say. If this is the best there is, then where are we with respect to the doctrine of reincarnation?"

**YOGI**: "There is other evidence, but you would find similar objections."

The frail Hindu, who was showing signs of restlessness, excused himself and went around to the back of the truck to irrigate the ground. Returning, he poured out another lemonade, added ice and salt, then spoke in a firmer tone.

**YOGI**: "My friend, it is like this. We in India have believed in reincarnation for thousands of years. It is in our scriptures, it is in our very bones. We don't need what you call objective evidence to believe in *karma* and rebirth. We accept it as a fact, an unquestioned fact, and are content to do so."

**VENDOR**: "Isn't that a trap, not to ask questions?" There was a pause. "Anyway ... go on."

**YOGI**: "We were talking about the American investigator, Ian Stevenson; and before that, I believe, about the progression of the soul toward perfection ..."

**VENDOR**: "Or perhaps regression? Isn't that possible?"

**YOGI**: "Well, yes, that can happen too. That's why perfection can take many, many rebirths. The process, theoretically, can be endless. It depends on the law of *karma*. Do you know about *karma*?"

**VENDOR**: "Yeah. Let's see. Your deeds in this life will determine the quality of the next. Right?"

**YOGI**: "Precisely. *Karma* will also influence the selection of an appropriate body for the next reincarnation."

**VENDOR**: "Mr. *Yogi*, perhaps you can set me straight on something? Do the Hindus believe that rebirth can happen in bodies other than human?"

**YOGI**: "Yes, indeed. Rebirth may be in a human body, or in an animal body, any animal. It is said that rebirth may be into a plant, or even into inanimate substance."

**VENDOR**: "Inanimate substance? You're kidding. You mean, like a rock? Like that lemonade jug?"

The Hindu was reminded of his thirst and reached for the container in question.

**YOGI**: "Yes, even reborn into this lemonade kettle."

**VENDOR**: "Jug."

**YOGI**: "Jug."

**VENDOR**: "Isn't that a little ridiculous? The jug is made up of a bunch of atoms. If each rock, each insect, each molecule or atom has a reborn soul, how many reborn souls are there?"

**YOGI**: "Ah, now you are asking a question which, I think, is impossible for me to answer."

There was an interlude while the lemonade man regrouped for a new approach.

**VENDOR**: "Mr. *Yogi*, you say that the cycle of rebirths, the Hindu doctrine of reincarnation, allows for spiritual evolution of the individual. One commits a crime in one life, makes up for it in the next. But look! We don't remember our past life. So ... ."

**YOGI**: "I agree. There is seldom a comprehensive recall ... ."

**VENDOR**: "...so, if I was a bad boy in my last life ..."

**YOGI**: "I know. If you have no recollection of your crimes ... ."

**VENDOR**: "... then how can I mend my ways? How can I atone? Is this reasonable?"

The vendor waved his hands in exasperation before adding some ice to the *yogi*'s lemonade.

**YOGI**: "Thank you, Sir. *Karma* is not an easy thing to understand. You may not have specific recall of past lives, but in your new life you are left with an awareness, an impression, a sensitization to the evil you have done."

**VENDOR**: "Aw, come on!"

**YOGI**: "Yes. If your *karma* brings you punishment, the suffering will have personal meaning for you. You will begin to recognize the virtues of compassion. In such a way, the individual progresses."

**VENDOR**: "Even if I bought that, there's another problem." He brushes a large black ant from the Indian's cup. "How can your idea of karma apply to a stone, or an insect? If the soul is trained by moral choice, what moral choices are open to that ant, or that jade ornament you' re wearing around your neck?"

**YOGI**: "I agree with you. Moral choices are thought to begin at the human level. That is why Hindu doctrine holds that the development of the soul is automatic until it is reborn in a human body."

**VENDOR**: "Then why would the soul of an ant not go directly to a human body instead of being reborn in, say, another ant? Wouldn't the whole process go a lot faster that way?"

**YOGI**: "We are dealing with the evolution of the soul. It goes slowly, the same as the evolution of the body. As you know, the human body has taken billions of years to evolve from primitive forms. Nature, apparently, is in no hurry with the body, or the soul."

The Hindu stopped the next question with an upraised hand, asking if he might excuse himself again in order to use the facilities around the back.

"There are no facilities around the back," corrected the vendor.

"I would like to use them anyway," smiled the Hindu, whose consumption of lemonade had been unrelenting. When he returned, it was the vendor who spoke.

**VENDOR**: "In Christianity, Sir, it is believed that the progression of the soul, after we die, takes place in our own body — our resurrected body, a *spiritual* body. And it takes place in Heaven, not on earth in a body of flesh."

**YOGI**: "You mentioned earlier that, in your opinion, the Hindu's reincarnation concept is based on speculation. Well, isn't yours?"

The lemonade vendor, in the interest of reordering his thoughts, changed the subject.

**VENDOR**: "That jade piece around your neck, Mr. *Yogi* — does it represent something special for you?"

**YOGI**: "You have a perceptive eye, my friend. Yes, this jade carving is a prayer piece. For me, it symbolizes Brahma, the Creator, my personal God. He is always with me."

**VENDOR**: "It's beautiful. I'd like to buy one like that as a souvenir of India. By the way, have you ever heard of the Saved Memory Hypothesis?"

The vendor extracts a book from the table drawer titled *Surviving Death*.

**YOGI**: "A gentleman was speaking to me about that book, oh — just last week, I think."

**VENDOR** (waving the book): "The Saved Memory Hypothesis says that decisions made in this life determine future states, just like *karma*. Did you read it?"

**YOGI**: "No. The gentleman that recommended the volume to me did not seem to regard the author's hypothesis as anything more than an idea to be falsified or verified as the case may be."

**VENDOR**: "Doesn't that assessment apply to reincarnation also?"

**YOGI**: "Perhaps for you as a Westerner. But the Hindu believer regards the cycle of rebirth as fact, not hypothesis."

The vendor thought he detected a touch of finality in the Hindu's tone, as though the dialogue might soon come to an end. Yet there were more questions to ask.

**VENDOR**: "Will you have another lemonade?"

**YOGI**: "I might have just one. Your lemonade is indeed excellent."

The vendor hastily refilled the other's cup.

**VENDOR**: "They say there are other things besides memories that bridge reincarnation from one body to the next. They say, for example, that special skills, likes and dislikes... phobias, language... even marks where a bullet or knife might have killed you in a previous life — these can show up in the next life."

**YOGI**: "True. We call that 'continuative karma'. You have been doing your homework, my friend. You seem well briefed for your college assignment. Now ... ." He makes as if to rise.

**VENDOR**: "One more thing, Mr. *Yogi*. In your theory, how does the soul ever manage to break out of the cycle of rebirth? Doesn't each life have its sins, requiring another rebirth?"

**YOGI**: "For some lives, the process would appear to be endless. For others, not quite so long. When escape comes, it is a release into bliss."

**VENDOR**: "What about Hitler? He has the blood of fifty or a hundred million people on his hands. Jews, gypsies, the sick, the war dead, burned out cities .... When does *he* step off the cycle of rebirth and unite with Brahman?"

**YOGI**: "Even Adolph Hitler, we suppose, had a soul ... ."

**VENDOR**: "Then let's take a case of pure, deliberate evil. Vlad, the Conqueror. You've heard of him? This guy got his kicks out of inflicting pain. He had pointed poles rammed up people's bums. He would sit eating his dinner with these skewered wretches planted around him, screaming their heads off. When one of his servants complained of the stink, he had him impaled on a higher stake above the smell. When does Vlad get off the cycle of rebirth?"

The Hindu did not answer immediately. He gazed silently at the ground, hands folded, his body quite still. Finally, he looked into the eyes of the vendor.

**YOGI**: "The questions of evil and suffering, my friend, have always been the most difficult questions to resolve for any religion. Hinduism, with its doctrine of reincarnation, usually associates evil with ignorance. To administer harm is to show ignorance of the feelings of one's brother, ignorance and absence of empathy for his point of view. In the cycle of rebirths, there is the opportunity to overcome this ignorance."

**VENDOR**: "That's fine for the perpetrator of the crime. Vlad gets to see his mistake, he's sorry and repents, he learns compassion. But what about his victims?" The vendor waves his hands in frustration. "All this incredible pain and suffering has taken place in the world, it is a historical fact! People and animals have suffered since life began on earth. It can't be taken away and returned to zero. Have they all committed crimes? Are there no innocent people? And Jesus! Why the punishment if they can't remember their crimes?"

**YOGI**: "There is no known answer, I am sure, to your very grave questions, my young friend. The enigmas of evil and suffering remain a puzzle. The derivation of evil and the purpose of arbitrary suffering have not been revealed to mankind. For a Hindu like me, the law of *karma* working through reincarnation is our best available example of moral justice. For you, there is Heaven and Hell. They have their own unresolved questions. Do the evil souls stay in Hell for an eternity? Is that the intent of a compassionate, merciful God? I have heard it said that your God, the Trinity, is either all powerful or all compassionate, but He cannot logically be both. Otherwise, why would He permit suffering to occur?"

**VENDOR**: "Mr. *Yogi*, your reincarnation concept is catching on in the West. People who once scoffed at the idea are now getting interested. You've heard of Shirley MacLaine's best selling books?"

**YOGI**: "Oh yes, I know the idea is gaining converts. I believe that the West's Heaven, Hell, angels, spirits, the last Judgment — these are becoming to some extent discredited in western society. They are considered, by many, to be at odds with science and modern life. Many Westerners are exploring the theory of reincarnation as a replacement for some of the traditional ideas. Many think of reincarnation as possibly a more credible alternative. Some respected Christian theologians — I give you Geddes MacGregor as an example — are finding a place in their system of beliefs for reincarnation. I'm sure you know that."

The vendor suddenly turned and cocked his head. "Customers coming, Mr. *Yogi*... they'll be thirsty." He got up from his chair. "Excuse me. Help yourself to more juice. I'll be back...."

A group of dusty travelers arrived, followed by a buzz of conversation. Orders were taken, and the young American poured energetically for the next quarter hour. When the rowdy band had left, he returned to resume his talk with the *yogi*. The Hindu, however, was not there. An empty cup stood on the table, and beside it was the green jade pendant, symbol of Brahma the Creator. The vendor gingerly picked it up and looked for the owner, but the *yogi* had departed and did not return.

# SPIRITUALISM, NEAR DEATH EXPERIENCE, & EXTRA SENSORY PERCEPTION

*Ghosties and Ghoulies and Long-Legged Beasties*
*And Things that Go Bump in the Night...*

"The Eagle has landed," radioed the lunar module as 'Buzz' Aldrin and Neil Armstrong touched down in July 1969 for mankind's first landing on the moon. This stunning achievement alone tells us that you and I are rather special animals. Yet, as we have seen, the well developed cerebral cortex that permits humans to outclass other animals in the thinking department also uniquely forewarns them that they must die. Humans may not know how or when they will meet with the grim reaper, but they are able to know that such a meeting will ultimately take place whether they like it or not. Thus, a conflict is created that we don't think other animals share. The conflict is between the instinct for survival and the awareness that survival is impossible.

What to do? Buzz Aldrin and Neil Armstrong presumably were not bothered by the conflict during their amazing descent to the moon's surface — they were too busy with the operation of their spacecraft. Distractions remove the specter of death from our attention. When we are less busy, most of us cope by denial. We speculate that we will continue to live in a spirit world after death even though there is no evidence for it.

But wait. A cult has arisen within the last century and a half that insists there is, indeed, objective evidence for the survival of the human spirit after death. This cult, which goes by the name of spiritualism, has had many respected followers, and claims to merit serious attention on the basis of the alleged 'evidence'. Spiritualism belongs to the category of the so-called paranormal. Literature on the subject overflows the shelves of bookstores devoted to the occult.

The word paranormal means beside, or beyond, the normal. It refers to the supernatural and has to do with such things as communicating with the dead, departing from the body when near death, and mind reading. Is the evidence for the paranormal credible, or simply an illusion? Let's take a look.

## SPIRITUALISM

Spiritualism is mostly about seances involving a 'psychic' medium who "channels" messages from the dead to an audience of 'sitters'. The dead may speak using the medium's voice, or the message may be written by the medium's hand, or come from table rappings or other sounds or signs answering questions from the audience. If it is a voice message, it is often received indirectly by being first passed from the dead person to another resident of the spirit world called a spirit guide or control who, in turn, channels the communication through the medium to the sitters.

Although the whole performance may bring a wry smile to the lips of some, it is taken very seriously by many exceedingly competent people. Included as believers have been such noted writers, scientists, and politicians as Sir Oliver Lodge, Sir William Crookes, Sir Arthur Conan Doyle, David Hume, Arthur Schopenhauer, Alfred Russel Wallace, John Masefield, Lord Tennyson, William Gladstone, J. J. Thompson, Mark Twain, William James, Lewis Carroll, and W. L. Mackenzie King. What convinces such astute people that spiritualism is legitimate? If we search for evidence, what do we find?

For starters, the audience of sitters is usually primed, emotionally cued, and ready to believe what is suggested to them. This charged atmosphere of expectation works to the benefit of the medium who is thereby enabled to give of his or her best performance. For example, if Sir Oliver Lodge, the physicist, comes to a seance in the hope of communicating with his dead son Raymond, he will not want to put the contact with Raymond at risk by carrying out a rigorous investigation of the procedure, the room, the medium, and the other people present.

Next, the medium is commonly a superlative performer, whether the acting is a deliberate fraud or whether it is natural without any intent to deceive. Most mediums of good faith and honest intentions have been reported by psychologists to be the victims of repressed conflicts resulting in mental dissociation and multiple personality. The multiple personalities reveal themselves during the trance, claiming to be spirits of the dead. The medium may have no conscious recall of the events of the trance, and be quite convinced that he or she possesses psychic powers. On the other hand, countless celebrated mediums have been exposed as tricksters, exploiting whom they may for fame or fortune. Such trickery has allegedly been perpetrated by such renowned psychics as Eusapia Palladino, Rudi Schneider, the Fox sisters, Ada Goodrich-Freer, and the exceptional Daniel Dunglas Home whom novelist Charles Dickens called 'that scoundrel Home', and poet Robert Browning labeled as 'Mr. Sludge the Medium'. For fraudulent practitioners, it is stock-in-trade to produce trumpets, accordions, grand pianos and people floating in the air, tables dancing about on the floor, or visions of dead spirits materializing out of 'ectoplasm', the supposed building substance of spiritual bodies. Harry Houdini, the masterful magician, denounced such mediums as 'human vultures'. There are few competent conjurers or hypnotists who could fail to produce these amazing illusions in a suggestible audience of sitters in a darkened seance room.

Suggestion, or some degree of hypnosis, certainly is known to play a prominent role in spiritualism. The legitimate medium is, according to psychologists, frequently the subject of self hypnosis. Psychologist T. W. Mitchell has written:

'One of the most remarkable features of deep hypnosis is the unexpected aptitude for dramatic impersonation shown by the hypnotized person. The literature of hypnotism is strewn with descriptions of the astonishing representations of well-known people given by hypnotized subjects in response to suggestion from without, and are rendered possible by some release of power, or freedom from inhibition, peculiar to the hypnotic state, so the character of a (spirit) control may be purely the result of self-suggestion by the medium taking effect in a self-induced hypnosis. If it is suggested to a hypnotized person that he is Napoleon Bonaparte he will accept the suggestion and will act the part; for the time being he appears to identify himself with Napoleon. So, if a medium goes into trance holding the conviction that he is controlled by the prophet Isaiah the trance personality will assume the title and play the part as well as he can. Some process of this kind would form the simplest explanation of the character of many of the ordinary controls of mediumistic trance, and it seems to me the most probable explanation of the imitation of the idiosyncrasies of dead friends seen in cases of 'direct control'.'

D. H. Rawcliffe has added:

'Despite the claims of the spiritualists and many adherents of psychical research, it can be amply demonstrated that the purported spirit personalities exhibited in the mediumistic trance display the same peculiarities as the secondary personalities witnessed in hypnosis, automatic writing or in certain hysterical phenomena. In a sentence, the 'spirits', 'controls' and 'guides' of the spiritualistic pantheon are nothing more than products of the medium's own mental processes. They are personifications or mirrored projections of the medium's own repressed impulses and wishes, moulded and conditioned by the ideas of spiritualism and the influences of the seance room.'

As for the sitters, their highly suggestible frame of mind is receptive to the hypnotic illusions and delusions created for them by the medium. We have only to see a stage hypnotist operate on a susceptible subject to be convinced that the hypnotist can produce in that person almost any delusion he wishes, making the subject see, hear, or feel the most outrageous and improbable things that, in reality, are not there.

Fraud, as practiced by spiritualistic mediums, is not always overtly intentional and may have complex roots. For example, a medium may begin a career believing in his or her supernatural gift but gradually drift into deliberate fraud to bolster a sagging performance or compensate for waning powers.

Belief in the paranormal phenomenon of spiritualism does not enjoy anything like the long, unbroken pedigree of the reincarnation hypothesis which dates back thousands of years. Although it has its origins in the shamanistic practices of tribal medicine men and witch doctors, modern day spiritualism probably made its formal debut only a century and a half ago when Margaretta and Kate Fox, two young American girls living with their parents near Rochester, New York, were reportedly able to summon up at will all sorts of mysterious knocks in the house which the family occupied. Subsequently they launched successful careers based on their supposed supernatural powers, but were eventually revealed as frauds.

From this bizarre beginning in 1848, mediumistic spiritualism spread like wildfire in seance rooms across Europe and North America, where thousands of professional mediums channeled messages from the dead to eager audiences. In 1882, the Society for Psychical Research was founded in England to determine if any evidence could be found for life after death, and in quick succession similar societies and associations were established in many other countries including the USA. The journals of these societies carry reports of thousands of supernatural events, often described in pseudo-scientific jargon, involving every sort of psychic phenomenon imaginable including the memory of past lives, the forecasting of future events, communication with dead spirits, mind reading, and the control of inanimate objects by thought power. There is an entertaining mixture of erudite discussion and simplistic fantasy in these reports, the bulk of which seems to consist of anecdotal stories and 'experiments' of dubious quality. None of this has made any serious impression on the scientific community or produced any useful result or verifiable information during the 110 years since the Society for Psychical Research began its investigations.

As noted by Rawcliffe: 'On scores of occasions intelligent investigators have testified unequivocally to their absolute conviction that such and such 'psychic' phenomenon took place which were afterwards proved to have been produced by tricks or mechanical means,' and, 'All the leading mediums who have been seriously investigated have been exposed as frauds at one time or another.'

The psychologist William James takes a non-committal position, siding with neither the pro, nor anti, spiritualists. He fudges: '... although ghosts and clairvoyances and raps and messages from spirits ... can never be fully explained away, they can also never be susceptible of full corroboration.'

T. H. Huxley, the biologist, was apparently of like mind, but was unconcerned as evidenced by his remark: 'It may all be true, for anything that I know to the contrary, but really I cannot get up interest in the subject.'

Although James and Huxley are both long dead, nothing seems to have changed since their time to sway the adherents of either camp — the believers are as credulous as ever, the critics as skeptical as before, and the vast majority of people remain, like Huxley, indifferent to the whole business.

## NEAR DEATH EXPERIENCE

In recent years there has been a flurry of renewed interest, particularly among New Agers, in the so called Out Of Body or Near Death Experience. The mental images and subjective impressions reported by some people who have been close to death have long fascinated followers of the occult. A common interpretation of these experiences is that the person involved is being given a glimpse of the supernatural realm that he or she will inhabit after death.

Let us suppose that somebody's heart and breathing have stopped as the result, say, of a bad accident, a near drowning, or during surgery. If resuscitation is successful and the person recovers, there may be recollections of leaving the body, floating above the accident scene or operating table, and watching with detached feelings as others work to revive the body. Commonly, there is a vision of bright light that radiates love and warmth, often appearing at the end of a dark tunnel or passage, drawing the disembodied person away from the scene. There may be dead relatives and friends hovering about, and the subject is frequently overwhelmed by a compelling wish to join them. The mood is one of peace and happiness, detached from space and time. There is no desire to return to the body but, regretfully, some sort of thread or cord eventually pulls the individual back. This is the sort of Near Death, or Out Of Body Experience reported by thousands of people whose accounts, although not identical, nevertheless contain some mix of the elements described above.

One of the most acclaimed investigators to systematically document Near Death Experiences has been Raymond Moody, an American philosophy student turned medical doctor. His first book, Life After Life, details many examples of Near Death Experience. Other methodical chroniclers of Near Death Experiences have been Sir William Barrette of the British Society for Psychical Research, Karlis Osis, Kenneth Ring, Michael Sabom, Edith Fiore, Maurice Rawlings, Margot Grey, and Elizabeth Kubler-Ross, each of which has compiled reports similar in nature to those of Dr. Moody, and each suggesting the operation of mystic forces to explain the reported phenomena.

It is, of course, always tempting when confronted with the mysterious or the unknown to ascribe to them a supernatural origin. We have already drawn attention in an earlier chapter to ancient mankind's belief in supernatural powers to account for thunder, lightning, and other manifestations of nature that were not understood. As mankind's information base and factual knowledge gradually grew, the real causes of puzzling events became apparent and humans accordingly began to jettison the gods which were becoming redundant.

In the same way, it is suggested that the mental images and subjective impressions of Near Death Experiences will ultimately find their correct explanation in the skewed processes of brain dysfunction, and there will be no reason to try and account for them by evoking the paranormal. In other words, Near Death Experiences may simply be the reflection of nerves and synaptic junctions that have been compromised by oxygen, glucose, and other chemical and physical imbalances causing a panoply of hallucinations. If Wilder Penfield, the well known neurosurgeon who mapped some of the brain's sensory and motor topography by poking at his patient's cerebrum during surgery — if Penfield were alive today, perhaps he would prod the brain some more to try and mimic the hallucinations of the Near Death Experience.

We are reminded by D. H. Rawcliffe that:

'... a genuine sensory hallucination ... invariably results from the dysfunction of the cerebral mechanism pertaining to sensory perception. The perception-mechanism of the brain starts operating of its own accord, as it were, without the external stimulus of light waves, etc., which are normally necessary for its operation. Such dysfunctions of the cerebral perception-mechanism are due to a number of different causes: amongst the more common are the effects produced by drugs, cerebral injury or disease, surgical operations on the brain, and different types of psychosis which result in deleterious changes in the cerebral functions.'

Rawcliffe further points out that:

'... in the out-of-the-body type of autoscopic hallucination — an experience cultivated by some mystics and divines and referred to as *ekstasis* by Plotinus — consciousness of self assumes a peculiar form. Instead of the subject retaining awareness of himself as he normally exists, i.e. with his sense of self inseparable from his body and its sensations, he sees an hallucinatory image of himself and simultaneously experiences the vivid delusion that this hallucinatory image is in fact his real self! This hallucination and its accompanying subjective delusion appear to be something like a dream in this respect, for in a dream it is not an uncommon experience to see oneself as if from a detached vantage point.'

Commenting on Near Death Experiences, the international news agency Reuters made this recent report:

'Near-death experiences probably result from the brain being starved of oxygen rather than from a glimpse into the afterlife, German researchers reported today. Dr. Thomas Lempert and a team at Berlin's Virchow University Clinic induced fainting by hyperventilation for up to 22 seconds in 42 healthy young volunteers. "Most subjects described the emotional experience of syncope (fainting) as pleasant, detached and peaceful, making them unwilling to return," the team said in a letter to the journal Lancet. Some compared it to drug and meditation experiences. One said: "I thought that if I had to die at this very moment I would willingly agree."' (Reuters, Sept. '94).

The point is, you don't have to be near death to have the mental visions and impressions of the Near Death Experience. They take place in certain abnormal states of brain function and may, or may not, accompany the dying process.

In view of the methodical investigation by qualified observers into thousands of reports of Near Death Experiences, there is no room to doubt that these subjective impressions do, in fact, occur. The disputed question, however, involves the interpretation. Are they spooky, or do they have natural causes? As of this writing, there seems no good reason to think that the Near Death Experience is a visit to the anteroom of a world beyond death.

## MENTAL TELEPATHY

Any discussion of the paranormal, however brief, would be incomplete without referring to the subject of mental telepathy which, along with clairvoyance and precognition, contributes prominently to the catch-all category of Extra Sensory Perception (ESP). Mental telepathy, thought transference, or more aptly 'mind reading', is defined as the communication between one mind and another by means other than the 5 senses. If you are in Tokyo and I am in New York, and you know what I am thinking, it is said to be by mental telepathy.

Do you buy it? Let's look at what happens when we think.

Thought involves a voltage drop sweeping along a nerve in the brain. When the voltage drop reaches a junction (called a synapse) with another nerve, the second nerve is stimulated to fire, or is inhibited from firing. Billions of such interconnected nerves, exciting and inhibiting one another, are required for thought to occur. The point is, thought happens inside the skull where the wiring is. Although electrodes placed on the outside of the skull can pick up brain waves, these waves seem to consist of background activity unlikely to be formed from components of thought. If they did contain thought patterns, there is no evident way that another person could receive and decode them.

Is there, then, any evidence for mental telepathy? Stage performers are able to put on an impressive show of mind reading, but the consensus of informed opinion to date is that these mind readers, without exception, are tricksters and do not actually read minds. Other examples of alleged thought transference are the stories we hear about someone who knows by mental telepathy of an event happening to another person, perhaps far away. Anecdotes, however, are not evidence. It is concrete proof that serious investigators of psychic phenomena have resolutely but vainly sought in countless telepathy experiments over the last hundred or so years.

One such investigator was Dr. Joseph Banks Rhine whose name has been almost synonymous with Extra Sensory Perception. Dr. Rhine, while head of the Parapsychology Laboratory at Duke University, and editor of the Journal of Parapsychology, researched telepathy (thought transference), clairvoyance (extrasensory knowledge of objects or events), and psychokinesis (displacement of matter by thought). Dr. Rhines's experiments using 'Zener cards' have received special attention by the public through his books.

His experiments involve an 'agent' or sender who sits at a table and looks at a series of 25 cards turned up one at a time from a shuffled deck. On each card is printed either a circle, rectangle, star, cross, or wavy lines. A second person who cannot see the cards tries to guess the symbol that the sender is looking at. Any score greater than chance is considered evidence of thought transference. The many thousands of trials by Dr. Rhine and others have shown that the number of correct guesses far outnumber those that could be expected by chance alone. Consequently, the experimenters have claimed that the existence of telepathy is a scientific fact. Actually, nothing could be farther from the truth.

The scientific community has never recognized as credible the experiments on ESP done by Dr. Rhine and others. The reason is the universally poor quality of the evidence that the experiments have produced. In not a single 'successful' telepathy trial has the minimum degree of control necessary to make the trial credible been imposed. When stricter control is exercised, the number of correct guesses becomes lower until, at the point where adequate control has been applied, scores are no better than chance.

Any experiment to prove thought transference must eliminate the passage of cues to the person who is doing the mind reading. This includes unconscious or involuntary cues issued by the well intended sender, as well as deliberate or fraudulent ones. There are many kinds of sensory cues that may be disseminated. Stage performers who are skilled at 'mind reading' rely on some or all of the following:

- Involuntary voice sounds and mouth movements
- Unconscious muscular movements
- Changes in facial expression
- Activation of vocal muscles
- Tension of facial and cervical muscles
- Ideomotor movements
- Alteration in rate, rhythm, and regularity of breathing
- Signals originating from others in the room

The majority of ESP experimenters have shown themselves to

be virtually unaware that one or more sensory cue sources could influence their results. It has been noted by Rawcliffe that:

'Unconscious observation and interpretation of sensory cues can be a very deceptive phenomenon, and there is no longer the least shadow of doubt that it occurs with many ESP percipients. It is deceptive in that *the percipient himself,* with his mind impregnated by notions of telepathy and other occult ideas, cannot recognize the true cause of his success in such experiments, and finds in these successes false confirmation of his own irrational beliefs.'

The ability to perceive and interpret faint sensory cues is sharpened to an extraordinary extent in some skilled people whether by natural aptitude, training and practice, sensory hyperacuity, or a combination of these. An obvious way to prevent cues from reaching the mind reader would be to place that person alone in a lightproof, soundproof, vibration-proof enclosure physically isolated from any conceivable outside signal and to use an automatic scoring device that would forestall any inadvertent scoring bias. Basic controls of this type have not been used in the work of such notable psychic researchers as Rhine, Soal, Chowrin, Kotik, Abramowski, Pagenstecher, Schmoll, Mabire, Wassiliewski, Tischner, Sinclair, and others. It would seem to be obvious to most, although evidently not to psychic researchers themselves, that an extra-sensory experiment should exclude any possibility of sensory signals reaching the percipient. In experiments where the mind reader is separated from his subject by large distances, the mind reading scores revert to no better than chance. Rawcliffe, who has examined the details of many ESP experiments as well as the credentials of the experimenters, offers the opinion that:

'The scientific world can never accept the claims of parapsychology until it has been convinced of the genuine scientific ability of the parapsychologists themselves, and until it is sure that the very highest scientific standards have been consistently applied...'

and,

'... telepathy and extra-sensory perception are nothing more than thinly disguised attempts to rationalize the occult, or else merely pretentious abstractions from primitive witchlore... however technological the jargon in which they are expressed.'

The lure of the supernatural is deeply ingrained in human nature and has long historical roots. Herewith is a list of terms arranged vertically in alphabetical order, that are associated with perceived happenings of mysterious origin. There is no horizontal correspondence between columns.

| PSYCHIC TERMS | COLLOQUIAL TERMS | ACTUAL CAUSES |
|---|---|---|
| astral projection | apparition | autohypnosis |
| channeling | exorcism | automation |
| clairvoyance | folklore | cryptomnesia |
| ectoplasm | ghost | delusion |
| ESP | haunting | fraud |
| levitation | medicine man | hallucination |
| medium | mind reading | hypnotism |
| metaphysical | miracle | illusion |
| paranormal | mystical | mental dissociation |
| parapsychology | myth | multiple personality |
| post-cognition | occult | naïve credulity |
| pre-cognition | poltergeist | neurosis |
| psi-gamma | possession | prestigitation |
| psychokinesis | prophecy | psychogenic hysteria |
| spiritism | shamanism | psychosis |
| spiritualism | soothsayer | sensory hyperactivity |
| supernatural | spirit | subconscious |
| telekinesis | superstition | suggestion |
| telepathy | voodoo | |
| thought transference | witchcraft | |
| transcendental | witchdoctor | |

Humans invoke a supernatural cause for things they don't understand. As Rawcliffe puts it: 'The human race as a whole has by no means escaped from its most primitive methods of thinking and turns toward the supernatural instinctively whenever its ignorance bars the path to knowledge.' He adds: 'To view the modern ESP movement in true perspective, one must realize that it is basically a cult – a cult of the supernatural in technical dress.'

The sheer volume of reports of the supernatural in journals of psychical research is overwhelming, but the analytical reader, unimpressed by quantity alone, is likely to disregard most of what he reads. Nonsense, whether in dribbles or torrents, whether garnished or bare, is still nonsense and of little value.

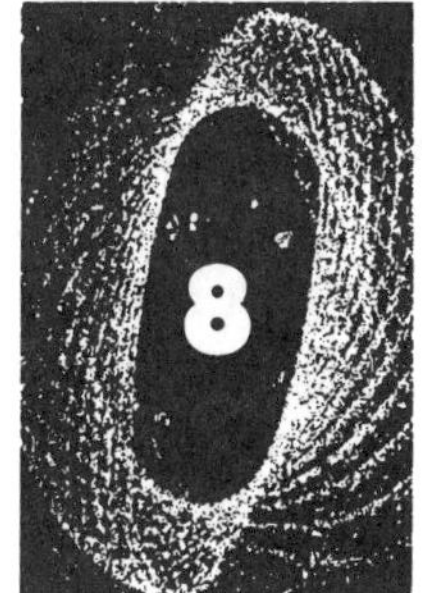

## THE INEVITABLE INTELLECT

Life has increased in complexity from the initial unicellular forms that populated this planet three or so billion years ago to today's human, complete with elaborate neural networks and an astonishing grasp of his or her environment. To be sure, the pace of progression has been painstakingly slow. A billion years here, a billion years there. But overall, the result is clear and undeniable — the production upon this planet of an intellect.

## TINKERING WITH EVOLUTION

An unprecedented point on the evolution graph has now been reached: mankind itself can finally intervene to change the course of its own evolution. Darwin and Mendel prepared the way for this startling event in the last century when they independently provided insights into genetic variability. Subsequently, Watson and Crick together discovered the structure of DNA and gave birth to today's rapidly maturing techniques of genetic engineering. Now it is feasible for humans to guide, or engineer, their biological destiny. They can do this simply by altering the DNA template from which they are constructed. An unanswered question lurks in the woodwork: what will be the consequences of this new found power?

We may fortunately anticipate that mankind's intentions will be to guide evolution toward the betterment of human welfare. But, 'the road to hell is paved with good intentions.' One person's welfare may be another's downfall. These are clearly areas where angels might fear to tread.

Is nature making a mistake by letting man tinker with DNA? Nature created this molecule, and passively permitted its evolution into mankind, the present end-point of biological complexity. No earthly intelligence was required to bring this about. Now, nature is allowing the brain of man and woman to take an active role in the shaping of evolution. Is this an error on nature's part? As far as we know, nature does not make 'errors'. Mistakes imply the frustration of a purpose and, as yet, no one has *identified* a purpose in this universe.

Strangely enough, mankind's new-found ability to shape evolution may cause it to eradicate the human species by bungling. As catastrophic as this would be for humans, it might be no great loss for the world. History shows that nature bypasses defunct species and is able to produce new and ever more complex forms. Dead ends and aborted experiments abound along the path, but a thrust toward the evolution of increasing intelligence seems to be nature's way. The world may lose people, but not necessarily intelligence. Indeed, intelligence should one day exceed its present development whether it is by the unassisted genetic engineering of nature, or the intentional manipulation of DNA by mankind.

**ALONE?**

Odds are that the planet earth is not alone in hosting intelligent life. Nature abhors uniqueness, so there are presumably many worlds like ours. One hundred billion or so stars stuff our local Milky Way galaxy, and about one hundred billion galaxies are moving outwards in the universe within range of our telescopes. This totals about ten billion trillion stars that we know about.

If one star in every hundred million was like our own sun with a planet that held intelligent life, then thinking beings may inhabit one hundred trillion worlds in the universe. Add Earth to make one hundred trillion and one. If there is any truth in the

Saved Memory Hypothesis, alien beings would be saved in addition to those from Earth.

Why don't we hear from any of these beings, some of whom may be a lot smarter than us? Because most of them would be billions of light years away. A signal sent from a world, say, ten billion light years away, presuming it was powerful enough to reach us (improbable), would arrive at Earth only today if it was sent ten billion years ago. The universe was young ten billion years ago, perhaps too young for intelligent life to have evolved. Our search for extraterrestrial life will be best limited to nearer distances, say, five billion light years (one light year is approximately six trillion miles) where the universe is more mature and life may have had more of a chance to start. This restricted distance greatly reduces the number of galaxies and therefore of candidates that we might hear from.

If we wanted to send a return communication, it would be wasted effort. Their world would probably be long gone by the time we received their message, let alone by the time they got our answer back. However, their message might contain something useful like how to cure cancer, stop war, or test the Saved Memory Hypothesis! The message would be no less useful if the senders and their world had been vaporized billions of years ago.

## SEEDING THE UNIVERSE

On Earth, life becomes ever more intelligent. At first glance, one might assume that intelligence must confer a survival advantage. It seems logical — the smarter we are, the better we can compete. Wrong. The assumption is not valid, for it can be seen that the lower forms of life, such as bacteria, have survived *on Earth* longer than us. Therefore, under present conditions, man has no survival advantage. But what will happen to the bacteria when Earth is totaled in a collision with another heavenly body? Or when the sun expands into a red giant and incinerates this planet? What will happen to life? Will intelligence give man a survival edge on a threatened planet?

Of course it will. Science fiction tells us how man might save the planet together with all forms of life from a potentially fatal collision with a very large meteor or asteroid: deflect the incoming body with a thermonuclear bullet. This solution is not without good theoretical foundation. There is also a potential solution to the red giant problem. When the kitchen (or the sun) gets too hot, get out of the kitchen. This also is theoretically possible. While man sails through space to more hospitable worlds, the bacteria will fry. Intelligence, then, seems to have a clear advantage.

Intelligence may be an attribute that, even as you read, is permitting life to seed the universe by space travel. The challenges involved in space exploration might be expected to exert selection pressure on intelligence that would foster its progressive evolution. A space traveler touching down on Earth today would probably overwhelm us with his smarts. And he might tell us that, without dissemination in space, life is restricted to spontaneous generation and early extinction in isolated regions of the universe such as our own. With dissemination, it survives and evolves.

## A CARPET OF LIFE

With our feet back on Earth, let's take another look at Earth's unit of life: the cell. In a later chapter, we'll peer at some of the cell's internal machinery. Now, let's talk numbers. How many of these little rascals are there on the globe?

To get a rough idea, I have just brought in an ordinary leaf from outside and measured its size. The leaf, composed entirely of cells, has an area of about forty square centimeters. After adding thickness (about a tenth of a millimeter), and estimating the volume of a leaf cell (a little over three thousand cubic microns), I calculate that the leaf contains one hundred million cells. That is, one hundred million individual units of life hanging from a stem. How many leaves are there in the world? How many roots, trunks, branches, blades of grass, microbes? Just to measure the cell numbers in a few square inches of grass would take a very dedicated numerologist a score of lifetimes counting at the rate of one cell per second. The Earth's continents and seas are covered with an almost continuous carpet of life in the form of such cellular units living free or attached to one another.

All of these units participate in the strange molecular dance of birth, death, and rebirth. The turnover can be counted in trillions of tons of biomass that die every year. The human being, of course, is part of the cycle. The Saved Memory Hypothesis postulates that only a small fraction of this biomass possesses any memory that survives death.

## IMPERMANENCE AND PERMANENCE

Twenty-five hundred years ago in northern India, the wise Buddha Gautama must have been contemplating the cycle of life and death when he concluded that the whole physical universe was impermanent. This insight, central to the philosophy of Buddhism, came to Gautama without the help of our scientific knowledge of decaying atoms, recombining molecules, or exploding novae.

Man is frightened by impermanence. He turns to religion and the occult to avoid it. He evokes the supernatural when objectivity fails him. The Saved Memory Hypothesis of this book concerns itself, like religion and spiritualism, with impermanence and permanence. It acknowledges the impermanence of this physical world, and proposes an extrapolated model that would allow for the continuity of awareness in another world.

Permanence and stability are illusory. As I write, I tend to think I am writing in a stable, fixed and permanent position in space. Not so. I am tearing through space on a spinning Earth that circles the sun. The sun, in turn, careens through a galaxy that speeds outward in an expanding universe. My spot is definitely not fixed.

Now, what about the objects around me? Everything appears so nice and familiar, and seemingly permanent. The room, the building, the people, the scenery ... WHAM! They could all vanish instantly in a catastrophic puff of thermonuclear smoke.

There is no permanence. Our material world is made of quicksand.

Yet intuitively we feel that this isn't true – that the world we know is somehow real and permanent, not just a crazy jumble of tumbling molecules. According to the Saved Memory Hypothesis, our intuition is right. The world with which we are familiar is permanent. So we have an apparent paradox: impermanence on the one hand, permanence on the other. But according to the Saved Memory Hypothesis, there is no paradox. Man's concept of reality is entirely subjective – real molecules impinge on his senses and create an image in his brain. The pattern of this image is instantly translocated to another milieu where it is immune to worldly catastrophe. When the pattern is reanimated, every impression, image, or construction ever held in the brain at any moment during life is recallable. Therefore, the chair on which I sit, the room, building, people, and scenery around me are all permanent even though they have been left behind or blown away. They are a permanent reality in my permanent, translocated memory despite the temporary nature of their original construction.

In an earlier chapter, we asked the question: On what grounds does mankind conclude that it, alone, will have existence in an afterlife, while other organisms will not? The Saved Memory Hypothesis gives man no special status among animals with memories as far as memory preservation is concerned. *All* memories are translocated from whatever living organism is biologically sophisticated enough to possess them, whether it be man, mouse, or mosquito. The leaf which I measured a while ago has, as far as we know, no mechanism for forming memories. Neither has a microbe. A memory that does not exist cannot be translocated. It is postulated, therefore, that organisms without memory will exist post-mortem only in the memories of those that have formed a mental image of them.

Theologian John Hick and philosopher H. H. Price propose a community of post-mortem centers of human consciousness whose members may be in some sort of telepathic communication. Dead minds, as it were, communicating with other dead minds. The Saved Memory Hypothesis also allows for this possibility but extends it to include all memory-endowed species. The degree of self awareness in individuals and species will *initially* correspond to the degree that was present on Earth. This means that whether you are human, dog, or lobster, your translocated self awareness will *initially* be no more, nor less, than it was during life. The word 'initially' is stressed, since change to awareness may be anticipated during the course of post-mortem 'life'. You can be expected to arrive like you are, but not to stay that way.

The community of centers of consciousness envisaged by Hick and Price seems to be one where the memory of each member is telepathically available to all; that is, all memories are shared by the community. This idea fails to fit with a basic assumption of the Saved Memory Hypothesis, which is that the memories of all organisms, not just humans, are translocated. If these memories were shared, a human might get a closer feel for a worm's predicament on a fish hook, or a lobster's problem with boiling water. But how could those animals, with their limited and specialized experience, make sense out of human memories of, say, a chess game, history lesson, or debate in Congress? A comprehensive understanding of a world reconstructed from the memories of all the diverse organisms that have lived in it through time would only be possible, it seems, in the mind of one who was capable of assimilating the individual experiences of each organism from its own point of view. If credit is given to the concept of an omnipotent Creator who could sense the total experience of every creature on Earth, then it may be supposed that He could reconstruct a world in His 'mind' that corresponded to the sum-total of all experience. This would be the world that we and our fellow creatures recognize as our own. Whereas the lobster cannot invent mankind's world, nor mankind the lobster's, the Creator might do both.

## SAVED MEMORY HYPOTHESIS VERSUS OTHER HYPOTHESES

The Saved Memory Hypothesis of this book does not stand in a vacuum. Other writers of this century such as Norbert Wiener, H.H. Price, and John Hick have suggested similar ideas. Our hypothesis endeavors to correlate such ideas with mankind's current knowledge of data storage, brain function, and quantum theory. It further offers the concept of incremental or continuous data transfer, not to an ethereal, phantom space, but to dimensions contiguous with the known universe.

Norbert Wiener, the cybernetics guru, has speculated about the 'transmission' of a body's pattern from one point to another. The concept became well known to fans of science fiction's Star Trek in which a device called a transporter ("Beam me up, Scotty") has the capacity to 'scramble' molecules at one location and reassemble them at another. Wiener wrote in 1950 that, '... there is no absolute distinction between the types of transmission which we can use for sending a telegram from country to country and the types of transmission which at least are theoretically possible for transmitting a living organism such as a human being.' This includes, 'the whole pattern of the human body, of the human brain with its memories and cross connections, so that a hypothetical receiving instrument could re-embody these messages in appropriate matter, capable of continuing the processes already in the body and the mind.'

In considering Wiener's ideas and their relation to resurrection of the body in the hereafter, John Hick raises the problem of the discontinuity of spaces. If this world is one space, A, and the hereafter is another space, B, with no physical connection between the two, then how can transmission by radio waves or other physical means occur between A and B? Hick suggests that it is difficult to account for this other than by 'divine' intervention.

The Saved Memory Hypothesis does not envisage such a problem, since it postulates that space A and space B are contiguous, not totally isolated from one another, and the concept of information transmission from A to B does not necessarily pose a theoretical obstacle.

Hick has another problem with Wiener's hypothesis. If one body 'replica' can be created, why not two or three? But he feels that such multiple recreations of the same identity would be impossible, since the same person cannot be the same if replicated into multiple copies.

The Saved Memory Hypothesis does not encounter this identity paradox because it distinguishes between body and Self. Replicas of the body can be, and are, created here in this world. Identical twins are body replicas, but they are not identical with regard to Self. The Self is a unique entity, not genetically created, but formed from stimuli received during life following conception. The Self of one twin, which is stored in the memory, is distinct from that of the other because the experiences of each are different. Hick might point out that Wiener's recreated clones include the replication of memory which is Self, so that we end up with a replication of what was supposed to be unique. The Saved Memory Hypothesis treats this point as a non-issue, since time does not stand still, and each replica, being subject to new and unique experience with time, acquires a separate identity or Self in the same manner that our own identity on Earth changes with time. In the case of multiple copies of a dead person being transferred to the hereafter, the similarities between the multiple Selves disappear as new experiences unique to each individual are acquired.

When Wiener's hypothesis of body transmission is thought of as the means of resurrection in a post-mortem domain, Hick visualizes still another problem. Suppose, postulates Hick, that a man expires from disease that ravages his body. When an identical body is recreated, it would no sooner reappear than it would expire again from the same causes. Hick seeks a way out of this dilemma by suggesting that an earlier, healthier body might somehow be the one that is transposed, or else the deranged body, when transposed, miraculously reverts to health.

The Saved Memory Hypothesis does not meet this problem because it does not propose the transposition of the earthly body after death. It presumes only the translocation of the memory pattern which is done, not only at the moment of death, but at all moments during life. Therefore, the memory of *all* bodies possessed from birth to death will be present in the hereafter. Although Hick tends to visualize the post-mortem world as having the same physical conditions and laws as the world in which we now live, the Saved Memory Hypothesis proposes a radically different milieu where the physical body to which our Self is now attached would neither fit nor function.

The possibility that the mind could exist without any body whatsoever has been seriously proposed by H. H. Price who offers reasoned arguments to support his thesis. John Hick comments upon this:

'Although the dualist belief that after bodily death the mind continues to live goes back in western thought at least to Plato, it has usually been a somewhat undefined belief... . The notion of the survival of the disembodied mind has long been in need of being turned into an intelligible hypothesis, and it is something of a scandal that it should have had to wait until the twentieth century for this to be done. However, it has now been done by the philosopher H. H. Price in a long and important paper, "Survival and the Idea of 'Another World'.

Three major elements of Price's hypothesis may be briefly stated as follows:

1. The afterlife is an elusive, disembodied, dream-like world based on memories of life;

2. Many inhabitants, between whom there is telepathic communication, share this dream-like world;

3. The recall and manipulation of memories is shaped by the desires of the dead individuals.

The postulates of the Saved Memory Hypothesis diverge from these three elements. In No. 1 above, Price seems to indicate a hazy world reminiscent of the shadowy Sheol of ancient Hebrews where dead spirits unhappily lurk. In contrast, the Saved Memory Hypothesis presumes that memories are so vivid that life can virtually be relived without distinction from the original experience. Price's hypothesis fails to indicate how memories might outlast the physical support of the brain, and where. The Saved Memory Hypothesis suggests that the physical pattern of memory is transmitted to a new, non-biological medium located in a contiguous environment of many dimensions. The new vehicle for the memory pattern is postulated to have brain-like or computer-like attributes that could fit and be activated in the post-mortem milieu.

John Hick points out that elements 2 and 3 of Prices' hypothesis seem to be mutually incompatible. A world shaped by the pooled desires of its individual inhabitants is not conceivable, since the preferences of one inhabitant would be in conflict with those of another. For illustration, Hick imagines a man and his devoted wife sitting comfortably side by side on the seashore, and notes: 'He might desire that they should be entertained by a troupe of dancing girls, she be quite content that they are not.'

The Saved Memory Hypothesis does not propose, as Price does, that the post-mortem world can be shaped by the desires of its population. Its precepts are closer to the views of Hick, who foresees an objective, externally imposed environment that has little to do with the desires of its inhabitants. The discipline of a world independently mandated by God is believed by Hick, the theologian, to be more conducive to the development of the soul than a world shaped by human desire.

A central plank of the Saved Memory Hypothesis is, like that of Price, the continuity of memory. But unlike Price, the Saved Memory Hypothesis postulates that this plank is only an initial part of a postmortem existence, an existence that is later enriched by the addition of fresh experience. This concept might please Hick, the theologian, who would see in it provision for maturation of the 'soul'.

## ACCOUNTABILITY — STUCK WITH THE BAGGAGE

Can we rationally conceive that we are accountable after death for our activities on Earth? According to the Saved Memory Hypothesis, we can, and the concept is simple. If we committed acts on Earth that caused us anguish, we take that anguish with us. The anguish, perhaps minimal on Earth, could progress following post-mortem reruns of our life to the point where it might simulate the torment of Hell. (Imagine Hitler and his colleagues with their fingers on the rerun button, learning to feel compassion for the millions whose suffering they caused by their own free will). Conversely, if our acts on Earth prove to be a source of joy, this too is baggage that we cannot jettison.

Billy Graham, the Christian evangelist, recently spoke to a large audience from a stadium in Germany. He looked aged and haggard, as though weighed down by a world that was breaking into pieces and landing on his own back. After a few remarks about global instability, he launched passionately into a discourse about the care of the soul. The soul, not the body, he said, is what survives death into eternity, so we'd better care for it extraordinarily well.

Billy Graham's message fits well with the concepts of the Saved Memory Hypothesis. Whether good or bad, all of life's experiences must be packed into our bags and taken with us. Past deeds cannot be forgotten, undone, edited, or selectively sloughed off. Past memories *are* the Self with which we commence post-mortem existence. We stand accountable.

It is further postulated that memories will not be passively watched the way we watch a 2 dimensional image on a movie or TV screen . We will *be there!* When we lived life, we lived it as sensory stimuli processed by the brain and lodged in memory. These impressions will be recreated in all their original detail to produce anguish and joy as if for the first time.

## COMPASSION

Compassion is the favoring of the welfare of others based on identification with them. Out of compassion comes the Golden Rule: 'Do unto others as you would be done by.' Compassion requires that we *identify* with the object of our attention such that, if the object is hurt, then so are we. Buddha said that what was done to his brothers was done to him. His 'brothers' included flies, which he would not swat.

Compassion is possessed to a varying degree by thinking beings. Jesus Christ, Mahatma Ghandi, and Mother Theresa spent their lives at it. Ghengis Kahn, Torquemada, and Jack the Ripper did not. Those who show compassion discriminate when they show it. A cat licks her kitten, but mauls a terrified mouse. A Roman enjoys the spectacle of a Christian being killed by lions, but stops on the way home to feed a beggar. Hitler was kind to his dog, but gassed millions of human beings.

Why does man show compassion at all? One answer is that it may confer an evolutionary advantage for survival. If you identify with your neighbor and give him help rather than a hard time, he is likely to become your friend and you won't kill one another. You will live to pass on your compassionate genes to your offspring.

A smoothly running human community presumably survives because of cooperation and lack of aggression between its members. An ant hill is different. True, you can have cooperation between ants in an ant hill without any show of compassion, but as you go up the ladder of brain development, cognitive compassion rather than instinctive cooperation becomes more common.

Compassion seems partly to be acquired by learning. Humans, unlike some other less sophisticated animals, have the brain potential to develop empathy, which is the basis of compassion. A child who, at the age of five, curiously pulls wings off flies and chops tails off tadpoles, may later abhor this behavior. He or she empathizes. Yet the majority of human beings have much of their potential for empathy undeveloped. Jesus knew this when he called from the cross: "Forgive them, Lord, for they know not what they do." Some individuals, despite learning opportunities, seem constitutionally incapable of eliminating or controlling their sadistic impulses. Society usually tries to protect itself from these predators, such as convicted murderer and torturer John Wayne Gacey, by jailing or executing them.

Society's evolution has shown a trend toward an increased expression of compassion. We see this in our religious teachings, in the evolution of laws respecting human and animal 'rights', and in the abandonment by law of many past barbaric practices. However, our halting efforts to establish justice, philanthropy, and kindness in earthly societies are often seen as inadequate and inconsistent. An example of such inconsistency would be Doctor Jekyll-Hyde who experiments on dogs, wears a raccoon coat, eats chicken and ribs, sets mouse traps in his basement, goes deer hunting, writes articles favoring vivisection, and finally sends a nice cheque to the Society for the Prevention of Cruelty to Animals.

The relevance of human compassion to the Saved Memory Hypothesis can only be conjectured in the sense that an individual's memory of his or her behavior towards other sentient beings will be the major part of the baggage he or she carries into a post-mortem world.

# DEATH

Death is indisputable, inevitable, and observable. It is, by definition, the end of life. Since death is an event that intervenes between life and a hypothetical afterlife, it bears further scrutiny here in *Surviving Death.*

**DEATH: WHERE, WHEN, AND WHAT?**

When a farmer chops the head off a chicken, the head drops to the ground, but the body may take off across the barnyard. Is the chicken dead or alive? At what point in space and time do we die? This is not as simple a question as it seems. In order to know where and when we die, we must ask: What is it that dies? What part or parts of the body?

**ONE CELL, MANY CELLS**

The death of a single cell, say the single-celled organism called the amoeba, is fairly straightforward. Death occurs when the cell structure is damaged to the extent that all activity ceases.

The situation is different in a many celled organism like a human being. We know that we lose billions of cells every day from our skin, intestines, blood, and other parts of the body. The cells die but we don't. That's because the remaining cells which form the greater part of our body continue to function as usual, and we as an entity survive.

## REMOVAL OF CELLS

Are we, then, dealing only with numbers? Do we have to count the cells detached from our body and arrive at a certain figure before death is pronounced? This, of course, would be nonsense. There is no magic number of cells that determines whether we live or die.

Each cell of the trillions in the body is self contained, alive, and potentially capable of independent survival after removal. For instance, blood cells may be transferred from our veins to a test tube where they will survive. Other types of cells from other places in the body may be put in a culture medium in a glass dish where, as in the case of some cancer cells, they may outlive the body from which they were removed. Not only can cells be transferred to test tubes or Petri dishes, but they may also be transplanted from one person to another. This transfer between individuals may be in the form of separate cells as in a blood transfusion, or sheets of cells as in skin grafts, or whole organs like a kidney or liver. Clearly, our cells don't have to reside in *our* bodies to live, and our body doesn't need them all to survive.

## THE BODY SPREAD OUT IN DISHES

It is evident, then, that the body can be taken apart, and the parts live independently. Theoretically, there appears to be no limit to the potential for dismemberment. If we give our imagination full rein, we can think of the removal and separation of all the cells of the body from each other, and their transfer into tubes, dishes, or the bodies of other living persons. Although the parts are alive and well, the original entity obviously has ceased to exist. The thing that was a person is no more.

Let's extend this thought further and imagine that the cells could somehow be brought together again from their scattered locations to reform the original body. We could then expect the reconstituted person to resume life as before. Does this theoretical exercise imply death and rebirth? Would it involve an escape of the Self to, and its return from, a post-mortem domain? It is the Self, after all, and not the scattered body cells to which we humans attach a high priority. We don't identify with cells, neither do we deplore their individual deaths.

## DEATH OF AWARENESS

Plato thought the Self, or soul, was in the heart. Descartes believed it was in the pineal gland. Today, our ideas are different. The study of brain structure, brain function, and brain disease has convinced us that the brain is the unique site of consciousness and Self.

What would happen to the sense of 'I' if the whole body were to be separated from the brain?

Such a macabre outrage, worthy perhaps of Dr. Frankenstein, was perpetrated early in the Century. The experiment involved the transplantation of the head of one dog to the body of another with the short term survival of the resulting hybrid combination. We would expect that, if the trauma of the operation did not impair brain function, a sense of awareness and memory might remain with the transplanted head in spite of its attachment to an alien body. Similarly, if a severed head were kept alive by a mechanical perfusion pump instead of by transplantation, we would not be surprised if there were a sense of awareness and memory retained by the perfused brain.

## SELF AWARENESS AND DEATH IN OTHER SPECIES

Some animals are smarter than others, and presumably have different degrees of Self perception to lose at death.

The brain of the human is far more complicated and can process much more information than the brain of a fly. The fly is mobile and resourceful but, unlike humans, could not design and construct a space ship or an electronic computer. We assume that the richness of awareness in people is due to their greater mental processing capacity, and that the sense of 'I' in mankind is both qualitatively and quantitatively greater than in a fly.

Proceeding backward in biological complexity, we find the lowly bacterium without any brain or nerves whatsoever, and presumably with no sense of Self awareness as we understand it.

Now eventually the fly, the human, and the bacterium will all die. If a bacterium has little or no sense of Self in life, then there will be little or none to lose at death. Perhaps this is why many people find it difficult to identify with creatures less complex than themselves and, unlike the Buddha, consider the death of a fly a matter of little or no consequence.

## MULTIPLICATION AND DEATH

Division of individuals prevents death of the species, but does little to preserve the identity of Self.

When egg and sperm unite to form a new generation, the parental cell parts and patterns are passed on. There is no passing on, however, of the Self. Though successive generations of similar bodies are made possible by DNA replication and cell division, there is no basis for the individual sense of Self to continue from one generation to the next. The Self in this world expires with the death of each organism.

## HOMEOSTASIS AND DEATH

We are not easy to kill. Our tenacious adherence to life is made possible by the 'homeostatic' mechanisms of the body which tend to counter any destabilizing threat. These homeostatic mechanisms work together in harmony like the department managers of a superbly run corporation to keep life intact.

Most homeostatic devices function automatically without our being aware of them. For instance, temperature, blood pressure, and heart rate are regulated by reflex homeostasis. On the other hand, some homeostatic mechanisms operate at a conscious level. We know they are at work when, for example, we feel anger, pain, or fear. These conscious feelings make us take action to adjust to our environment and keep harm away. The ultimate destabilizing threat is death, and all homeostatic mechanisms are geared to oppose it, both at the conscious and automatic level.

## AGING AND DEATH

In the last century or so, life expectancy in many areas of the globe has doubled. This happy circumstance has been brought about largely through the control of infectious diseases. However, humans would like to live even longer and in perfect health. This will be difficult, because the universal process of aging causes destructive changes to the body that accumulate, interfere with function, and eventually kill the body.

Ponce de Leon thought there might exist a fountain of youth in which he might bathe. He searched assiduously for it without success. Later, the French physiologist Brown-Sequard tried to avoid aging by injecting himself with extract of monkey's testicles. Despite exaggerated claims of efficacy, this didn't work either.

Today, many scientists believe, like Ponce de Leon and Brown-Sequard, that the termination of life by aging is not inevitable. In the last half of this century, a great rolling snowball of investigation into the biology of aging has taken place. These efforts have contributed to our knowledge of the body to an impressive degree but, as far as breakthroughs in longevity are concerned, no cigar!

All the body systems degenerate with time. This includes respiratory, cardiovascular, renal, digestive, sensory, and other systems. Old people just don't function very well. Although we begin life with excess capacity in most organs (we can get along on one kidney or lung quite well), this reserve is steadily eroded as the years roll by. As one system or organ degenerates, greater demand is put on the others. Eventually something gives. A system runs out of steam as its reserves are depleted, the body can no longer cope, and everything shuts down in death. This is considered normal aging.

Why this relentless degeneration? When we are young, we get growth, not degeneration. It is only later that breakdown beyond the capacity to repair supervenes. 'Catabolism' overwhelms 'anabolism' and we get old. What causes this changeover?

The obvious reasons for tissue breakdown are injury and disease. The damage from these disturbing factors accumulates with age. But there are probably other, more obscure reasons for aging. These may consist of DNA programs that are translated into the destructive alterations found in aging tissues.

The wide differences between the life spans of various organisms is puzzling. Mouse and human are both products of relatively recent evolution, and they have closely related anatomical structures. Yet a mouse is old and ready to die at 3 years, whereas humans can live to be over 100. The reason for this discrepancy is not known, but since the structural differences between mouse and people that determine longevity occurred over a relatively short period of evolutionary history, they are probably of minor magnitude and susceptible to manipulation. Thus, a biological breakthrough that slows down, or stops, aging and thus greatly extends human life will probably involve gene manipulation, and seems entirely feasible. It would doubtless be eagerly accepted by many individuals because of its rewards and despite its problems. By avoiding aging, however, we will obviously not prevent death. Even without senility, death, like taxes, will overtake us eventually.

## LIFE SUSPENSION BY FREEZING

At this point, it may be relevant in our discussion of death to examine the idea of the *suspension* of life as opposed to its termination. Can biological life be stopped, and started again? If so, are we experiencing death when life stops, and do we return from death when it restarts?

Life, in so far as it has to do with metabolic activity, is influenced by the *rate* of cell metabolism, and this in turn is governed by temperature. If we could reversibly stop metabolism by chilling, we could suspend life. Examples of slowing, but not stopping, an organism's metabolism are commonplace. We refrigerate food so that contaminating bacteria will be chilled, won't multiply, and won't give us food poisoning from their toxins. Again, winter temperatures chill the cold blooded bodies of frogs or snakes, and the animals become dormant as their metabolism slows down. Finally, organs harvested for transplant are routinely cooled in order to retard their cell metabolism and thereby reduce their need for circulating blood prior to connection with the blood supply of the new host.

What has all this got to do with the *suspension* of life? In the above examples, the chemical and physical processes in living cells were slowed down by moderate cooling, but not stopped. Now, what would happen if the temperature were to be lowered to the point where all intracellular activity ceased, where each molecule in each cell virtually stood still? Would we not be left with an inanimate object, as lifeless as a piece of glass? If the frozen cells were subsequently rewarmed, would we not expect normal activity to return to the cells?

The answer at present is a theoretical yes, but a practical no. An animal that is chilled to the point where cellular metabolism is totally arrested will form internal ice which rips the tissues and cells apart, quite beyond repair. Thus the cells, and therefore the animal, can no longer support life.

This is not the end of the story, however. We see plants and animals all around us in the wilds of nature that routinely survive the sub zero temperatures of winter. Even after a severe winter season, spring emerges with its blooming vegetation, biting insects and croaking frogs. How do these life forms avoid death from freezing? To answer this question, let's take a little side trip into the world of cell dynamics when the mercury outside dips below zero degrees Fahrenheit. We will see how nature slows, but does not stop, metabolism in freezing weather.

When ice forms in the body, it forms first in the body cavities (bladder, stomach, et cetera) and in the 'interstitial' fluid between cells. It is this interstitial ice that does the irreparable damage to the body. The ice crystals draw water out of the cells by osmosis and cause the cell to collapse, its surrounding membrane to rupture, and the cytoplasm and organelles inside it to spill out. The drama concludes with the death of the cell and, if the freezing is extensive, the death of the host.

How, then, do plants, insects, and life forms that remain above the ground survive winter? There are two principal methods.

The first is to prevent ice formation. Some organisms are able to do this by the elimination of small particles in the fluid outside the cells on which ice crystals initially form, and by the synthesis of antifreeze molecules which lower the freezing point of body water much as we lower the freezing point of water in our car radiators by adding Prestone.

The second method is to prevent ice damage by ensuring that, if ice crystals form, they form slowly and remain small. The organisms that have evolved this method of protection accomplish it through the synthesis of a variety of proteins, alcohols, sugars and amino acids which promote early ice crystal formation, restrict the size of the crystals, protect the cells against osmotic shrinkage, and stabilize the cell membrane against rupture. Nature's life forms, then, have evolved different and efficient techniques for surviving their winter habitats. You might go out in the month of January in the state of Montana and find a frog under the snow on the forest floor. Examining it, you would note that the body cavities were filled with ice, and observe the heart and lungs to be quite still. If you took the frog inside and gradually warmed it up, however, that frog would croak and hop with the best of them! Nature won't let her species freeze to death.

A check on the cellular metabolism of the frog in its chilled state would have revealed that the physical and chemical reactions in the semi-liquid interior of its cells were slower than normal. Some frozen animals can survive the winter with their cellular metabolism retarded to within a few percent of normal. Thus, nature reduces the activity in chilled cells and, at the same time, protects them from ice damage.

Nature, however, does not stop metabolism entirely. Human researchers, on the other hand, are able to do this. In 1949, they first froze sperm cells in a glycol antifreeze solution and later revived them. Since then, improved methods of cryopreservation have evolved which now include flash freezing techniques that can instantly and reversibly vitrify a cell to a glass-like consistency without damaging the cell architecture.

One would expect that such advances in cryopreservation would promise a bonanza for those interested in conserving organs for transplantation. Visions emerge of tissue and organ banks around the world replete with frozen hearts and livers ready at a moment's notice to transplant into needy patients. Regrettably, this is not the case, at least not yet. Workers so far have been unable to cool and rewarm whole organs without injury, or to perfuse large tissue masses with cryoprotectants without damage to the cells. Current freezing techniques are nevertheless successful and applicable to individual cells such as sperm or fertilized eggs, and to simple tissues like flat skin layers.

If whole organs cannot be frozen without fatal tissue damage, why do some people pay a hundred thousand dollars or more to have their bodies, or heads, frozen at death in liquid nitrogen? They do it expecting that they may be thawed out, revived, and restored to health when, and if, new discoveries should make that possible. Unfortunately, there appears little hope of reviving a body whose delicate cells and tissues have been ripped apart by ice crystals or destroyed by chemicals. Evidently both the body temperature and bank accounts of such individuals will be lowered without any compensating increase in longevity.

## DISTINCTION BETWEEN DEATH AND LIFE SUSPENSION

Is there a difference between life suspension and death? If we cool a cell to the point where all the molecules stand still while at the same time avoiding damage to the cellular architecture, is the cell dead or alive? If the cell can be revived, we fudge the answer by saying that its life is 'suspended'. Whether or not the stilled molecules are able to resume their normal motion again will determine the name we give to the state. Even if the cells were frozen for a billion years, we would still think of it as having suspended life if it were revivable. The distinction between death and life suspension, if it exists, is certainly not apparent.

## LIFE SUSPENSION BY OTHER METHODS

Although cooling is perhaps the most obvious method that comes to mind for slowing down or arresting metabolism in cells, it is not the only means. The rate at which a molecule accelerates is not merely a function of temperature, but also of mass. If the mass of a molecule in a cell is increased, its relative motion will slow down. How might we increase the mass of the molecule to the point where its movement would stop?

Einstein in his Theory of Special Relativity calculated that the increase in the mass of a moving body becomes very great, reaching infinity when the velocity of the moving body reaches the velocity of light, according to the equation:

$$m = \frac{m_0}{\sqrt{1 - \frac{v^2}{c^2}}}$$

where m stands for the mass of a body moving with velocity v, $m_0$ for its mass when at rest, and c for the velocity of light. Thus, by increasing the velocity of a moving cell close to that of light, its mass approaches infinity, the movement of its molecules slows to a virtual stop, and life is suspended in that cell. What would apply to a single cell would also apply to a human being made up of many cells. We would expect that the metabolism of a human body moving close to the speed of light would approach zero and life would be virtually suspended. If such a person were riding in the starship Enterprise at 'warp speed', he or she could not function as a crew member unless the space ship slowed down and allowed the molecules in the body to start moving again.

The length of time that life is suspended, whether by chilling or high speed travel, should not affect the capacity of the organism to revive. Whether a person's life were suspended for a year, or a billion years, his or her condition and physiological age on reanimation would presumably be the same as it was at the beginning of the experiment. The universe, however, might be a billion years older.

Other methods for the suspension and reanimation of life such as dehydration and rehydration are theoretically possible and potentially useful. Although the distinction between death and suspended life may not be clear, the philosophical ambiguity won't slow the laboratory search for improved methods of life suspension and organ preservation.

## THE NECESSITY OF DEATH

If we didn't have death on this planet, the human race would not be here. Primitive organisms multiplying exponentially would have filled all available space long before higher organisms, like ourselves, could evolve.

Even with death and contraception, our planet is starting to get crowded. However, should men and women succeed in leaving Earth, and spread themselves around in the wide spaces of the universe, then death may no longer be required to make room for their children.

# LIFE

*Fact No. 1:* A society of cells has come into being that, through intense cooperation, has built me a brain.
*Fact No. 2:* This brain is able to study itself and its environment.

The author's brain invites the reader to join it in briefly examining the cellular life that supports all living tissue, including itself.

**WHAT IS LIFE?**

The term life is not easy to define. Whatever one says about it, there always seems to be an exception. According to one dictionary definition: 'Life is a state of ceaseless change and functional activity peculiar to organized matter.' Does this definition help us? What does this *ceaseless change and functional activity* refer to?

Such a definition does not apply to a frozen cell which, although it may be 'alive', is not in 'a state of ceaseless change and functional activity' until warmed up. On the other hand, we can think of non-living objects that do conform to the definition. For example, a car's engine is organized matter and clearly in a state of ceaseless change and functional activity as its pistons shoot up and down, sucking in and burning gasoline as it propels the car along the road.

What, then, is life? How do you and I, who are alive, differ from the automobile, which is not? To posses life, an object is expected to do at least 3 of 4 things:

1. reproduce itself;
2. move about;
3. respond to stimuli;
4. metabolize.

Further, it is anticipated that these activities will be self-generated. The amoeba, like countless other single celled creatures, is capable of performing all 4 of these activities. It reproduces by dividing, moves about by extending pseudopods, responds to stimuli by contracting, and metabolizes ingested materials.

Not all of these 4 attributes need be present for life. For example, *reproduction* may no longer be possible in a cell overdosed with radiation. Again, it is not feasible for a tree to *move* from one place to another. Neither will a person *respond* to stimuli when he is properly anaesthetized. Yet, in each case, the object is alive.

In contrast to living things, matter that is not alive may show one or more of the 4 attributes, but not most of them. For example, there are inanimate molecules able to *replicate* themselves in a test tube, robots that *move*, and bubbles that *respond* if pricked. Yet, less than 3 of the 4 attributes of life are present in each. The objects are therefore not considered to be alive. In the case of the frozen cell, the 4 attributes are 'suspended', and life is potential.

Pondering questions of life and its meaning is, of course, the bread and butter of philosophy and religion. For most of human history, philosophers and priests have addressed such matters by guesswork or anecdote. Only in the last couple of centuries has science totally changed this situation. Mankind can now examine the physical processes that constitute life in the most minute detail at the microscopic and biomolecular levels. Progress is also being made in relating the mental aspects of life, that is, consciousness and psychological processes, with brain activity. Our understanding of life's mechanism is expanding in ways that neither Moses, nor Aristotle, ever dreamed of.

## THE CELL AS LIFE

An English gentleman named Robert Hooke looked through his microscope (just invented) at a piece of cork in the year 1665. He noted with only passing interest that the cork was riddled with tiny empty spaces. He christened these spaces *cells*. Little did Hooke suspect he had discovered a fundamental unit of life. Although a simpler biological object, the virus, exists, its status as a living organism is controversial. The cell, on the other hand, fully qualifies as a bona fide life form. Its highly organized structure can replicate, metabolize, respond and, if unattached, move around by its own power.

In the centuries following Hooke's discovery, microscopes and methods of preparing cells for study got a lot better. It soon became apparent that the cell is an incredibly complex entity, not just an empty space or bag of inert material. It is a finely structured, miniature factory in which thousands of stunningly intricate and interdependent processes take place. These are the processes of life, encapsuled in tiny envelopes much too small to see with the naked eye. Today's researchers employ advanced tools and techniques to pry into the cell's astounding secrets. These methods, such as electron microscopy, ultra centrifugation, and radioautography have enabled us to take life apart and see what makes it tick.

## WHY DO CELLS EXIST?

Specialization requires separation into distinct units. This is clear when we look at the things around us. They are packaged. Television sets, automobiles, houses, ships, cities: they all have boundaries that enable them to perform their unique functions.

The concept of specialization and boundaries applies to living substance as well. Protoplasm, the substance of life, owes its existence to the cell package that contains it. The protoplasmic gel is bounded by the cell membrane and so remains separate and distinct from the protoplasm of neighboring cells. Separation makes uniqueness possible. The differences between unicellular organisms such as amoeba and paramecium exist because their protoplasm is not merged.

Organisms with many cells, like the human being, show intense specialization among their individual cells. For example, muscle cells contract, gland cells secrete, intestinal cells absorb, nerve cells transmit.

**LIFE IS WORK**

The 'ceaseless change and functional activity' referred to as life by the dictionary boils down to the shuttling back and forth of molecules inside the cell. The nuclear fires in the sun, 93 million miles away, indirectly provide the energy for this activity.

Our cells, then, are anything but lazy. Whether we are awake or asleep, they push particles around in a continuous frenzy of activity. The cell is like a busy factory operating all shifts where the workers never stop for holidays or strikes.

The result of the cell's intensive labors is simply to maintain itself and its host in a functioning state. To this end, endocrine cells make hormones, blood cells make hemoglobin and antibodies, muscle cells make contractile proteins, pancreas cells make enzymes, and so on. The point is, each cell is a specialized workaholic. If a molecule in the body is not made by the cell, at least it is probably taken into the cell, pushed around, and modified. As busy as the cells are during sleep, imagine their stepped-up activity when we run for a bus or build an Egyptian pyramid under demanding taskmasters.

Nothing moves unless it is moved by energy. Where does an animal cell get the energy for its molecule pushing? Indirectly, from the sun. More directly, from chemical reactions that take the resting, or potential, energy contained in food and convert it into the kinetic energy, or energy of motion, that the cells require. By analogy, we burn gasoline in our cars, converting its potential energy into energy of motion which pushes the pistons and turns the wheels. The cell, instead of burning gasoline, burns sugar, fat, and protein with the same useful result: the conversion of potential energy to kinetic energy.

## WHEELS WITHIN WHEELS

Specialization in the cell, of course, requires a division of labor. The interior of the cell, far from being everywhere the same, is populated by many different structures called organelles. The organelles are like machines in a factory, each suited to its own particular job. If you mixed the cell contents all up together with no separating boundaries, specialization inside the cell would be a hopeless task. For instance, a chemist who wants to carry out two separate chemical reactions does not mix all the ingredients together in the same flask. He uses two different flasks and keeps the reactions from interfering with each other. The cell uses the same strategy. The chemical ingredients inside the cell are kept apart by the specialized intracellular organelles.

Cell organelles are many and varied. They are the structural units that make it possible for the chemical and physical processes of life to proceed. They go by such names as nucleus, Golgi apparatus, lysosomes, mitochondria, smooth and rough endoplasmic reticulum, coated vesicles, microtubules, and micro filaments.

Some of these organelles were first seen with the light microscope which could only reveal vague outlines and fuzzy shapes. In the 1930's, the electron microscope was invented, and the precise structure of the particles soon leapt into view. Shortly after came information about how organelles work. Tools such as radioautography, which shows where different substances in the cell are made, and ultracentrifugation, which separates organelles from one another and reveals their contents, enabled investigators to enter this busy factory called the cell and take a good look around. They could now watch the machinery work.

## WHERE THE CELL'S USABLE ENERGY COMES FROM

The reader is now invited to return to our unfinished story about energy. Having talked about organelles, let's meet one.

It's called the mitochondrion, and is an important player in the way usable energy is made in the cell.

Mitochondria are commonly shaped like sausages, and time-lapse photography shows hundreds of them scampering around inside the cell like little submarines, going wherever energy is most required. Useful energy is produced inside the mitochondrion by a process called oxidative phosphorylation, a big name for an important reaction that uses oxygen from lungs to make high energy molecules called ATP. Enzymes, lined up inside the mitochondrion, pass electrons from one to another like firefighters in a bucket brigade handing on pails of water to put out a fire. By this cooperative process, usable ATP molecules are synthesized and stored in the mitochondria like drums of gasoline ready to be burned in an engine. The cell can break down these high energy ATP molecules whenever it wants to do work. Without this energy from ATP, the cell could not function and would die. For the interested reader, more details about these reactions may be found in Appendix II.

Our cells can shift gears and obtain additional energy from other chemical pathways which kick in when oxygen is in short supply as, for example, when sprinting. These alternate pathways are far less efficient sources of energy and are not adequate by themselves for sustaining human life. However, simpler organisms that have not evolved a better way of obtaining energy may use such pathways exclusively.

We may note in passing that some Nazi officers during World War II chose to end their lives by stopping oxidative phosphorylation in their cells. The standard issue of suicide capsules, it seems, contained cyanide, a chemical that prevents oxidative phosphorylation from taking place. When the user swallows it, he can expect to die in seconds. Field Marshall Erwin Rommel, the 'Desert Fox', died this way as did Hitler's wife, Eva Braun.

## AN INCREDIBLE DANCE

The cell is not only productive, but astonishingly skillful into the bargain. The way it makes protein is a good example of its engineering skills.

If we imagine ourselves entering a cell, we immediately notice that there are protein molecules all about us in the process of being fabricated. Since proteins are made from smaller molecules called amino acids, it is not surprising to see these little rascals lurking in the wings, as it were, like shy maidens waiting for a partner with whom to dance. Some of the amino acids, impatient for action, are seen to lock hands in a conga line which gradually gets longer. This is as it should be, for they are constructing a protein, and a protein molecule is basically nothing more than a long string of amino acids connected end to end.

'Arthur Murray will teach you dancing in a hurry,' goes an old song. All very well for Arthur Murray's students, but who taught amino acids how to dance? Which amino acid should go where, and in what order?

Fortunately, there is a molecule in abundance in the cytoplasm called m-RNA which, like Arthur Murray, creates order out of chaos among the dancers. The different amino acids line up along the m-RNA molecule and attach to it in a definite sequence matching an m-RNA code handed down by DNA. By locking hands, the dancers form a chain of increasing length. When their chain is complete, it is released from the m-RNA as a bona fide protein. Additional details of this amino acid dance, fundamental to life and stopped by death, may be obtained by the interested reader from Appendix III.

We have seen in barest outline some of the work of the cell. But the synthesis of ATP and protein, upon which we have touched, are only two examples out of thousands of cellular reactions going on at the same time. The life processes in each minute cellular laboratory are the most complex known on earth. Little wonder they have been evolving for billions of years.

A feature of the activity in a cell is the fact that the chemical pathways overlap and interact. Perturbation theory suggests that a butterfly's wings flapping in China may be felt around the world. In the same way, each molecular event in the cell sends out ripples that are felt by other cellular molecules.

The directions that guide intracellular reactions originate in the genes, that is, in the DNA of each cell. These instructions do not change from one cell generation to the next, except when genes mutate. Normal instructions incorporate checks and balances like those we see in the government of a democratic society where one governing branch is supposed to counter the excesses of another. In the cell, escape from this control can create the havoc that is seen in cancer. A mutation in a gene that normally brakes growth, or in one that selectively accelerates it, upsets the checks and balances and unleashes uncontrolled cell division that causes the death of the host.

There appears to be nothing strange, mysterious, or in any way supernatural about life in the cell. There are no spooks or evident influences from other worlds. The processes we observe are predictable chemical reactions based on known causes and effects. The hand of God may be directing this life but, if so, it is in accordance with the same laws that direct the rest of the universe.

When death brings an end to life, it throws a monkey wrench into the cell machinery. In a multicellular organism, not all cells succumb simultaneously, as may be noted by hair and nails which continue to grow on a corpse. We speculate that cell organelles, when they die, don't go to heaven or hell. If they did, it is unlikely they could function there, for they are made by, and adapted to, this world where they have gratuitously created our memories and consciousness. It is the latter which, according to our hypothesis, may continue to exist after death.

**CAN LIFE BE CREATED IN THE LABORATORY?**

Is there any way that you or I could create life in the lab? Start it, that is, from basic elements and simple compounds — the same raw materials that nature presumably used about three and a half billion years ago when she created life on earth? Efforts have been made in the laboratory to duplicate nature's early success, but all such attempts have failed. This does not mean that scientists are doomed to perpetual failure. Frankenstein's fictional monster is a brain that lived, died, and lived again in another body. This is not creation, but merely the continuation of life in a structure already built. What about creating life from scratch by combining simple, inanimate molecules into structures with the properties of life?

Biochemistry teaches us that the human body is composed of only a few chemical elements, the same elements that make up most other objects in the universe, whether animate or inanimate. It is the way that these elements are put together that enables the resulting structure to support life. Maybe such a structure could be synthesized in the laboratory, perhaps using as a model some simple unicellular organism found in nature. This would require exact knowledge at the molecular level of all components of the life model, and methods not yet invented for putting the parts together. If the final synthetic object was identical to that which nature produces by means of cell replication, we would expect it to act like the real thing. And if a simple life form could be created in the lab, it is conceivable we could learn to put together more complicated forms — even those with neural networks, memories, and a perception of Self. None of these manipulations would violate any natural law of our universe. Any laboratory synthesis would have to be conducted within the same framework of natural law that governs the synthesis of life by spontaneous generation in a primordial soup or by its subsequent genetic replication. The concept of God as ultimate creator is not challenged by the exercise of laboratory ingenuity on the part of mankind. However, it is not clear what purpose would be served by the creation of biological life in the laboratory from inanimate materials, nor is it predictable to what extent it would be tolerated by a religious, conservative, and wary society.

Even if synthetic biological life were attempted, the probability of success would be remote. Life's tortoise-like progression from the first mysterious pre-cellular forms to the complex structure that we now recognize as the cell may have taken two billion years or so to achieve. It would be astonishing if laboratory methods, no matter how impressive, could accomplish this miracle of nature overnight. More likely will be the emergence of a mechanical counterpart to the human body endowed with advanced, computer-based intelligence. In view of its potential usefulness, there is little reason to expect serious opposition to the invention and construction of such devices. Undoubtedly, opinions will differ as to whether they are alive or not.

# FROM THE BIG BANG TO THE BIRTH OF LIFE

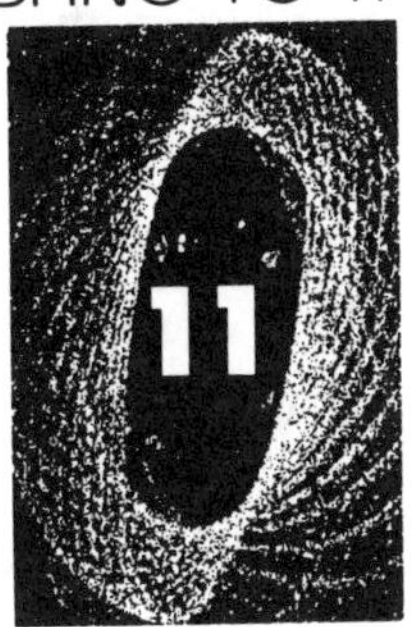


## PART I: THE COSMOS

### IN THE BEGINNING

Relatively speaking, humans are smart and proud of it. In less than a hundred years, they have found answers to such difficult questions as why the stars burn and how the Earth was formed. But the biggest question of all is still open: How did the universe come to be?

Theologians, of course, see no enigma. "God did it," they say. How? "By a divine act." Scientists, who don't like loose ends, would prefer more detail. They want chapter and verse, but not according to Genesis.

In this search for specifics, one school of scientists proposes a 'Big Bang' theory, whereas another group favours a 'Steady State' theory. As the names imply, these 2 theories are in conflict.

The man who made the original observations that gave rise to both theories was the late astronomer Edwin Hubble. This celebrated man discovered in the 1920's that the heavens are populated with galaxies (clusters of billions of stars) and showed that these galaxies are speeding away from one another, the farthest traveling the fastest (at up to 90% the speed of light). Hubble saw that the universe appeared to be expanding like a rising cake where space is the dough and galaxies the raisins.

Hubble's vision conveyed to nuclear physicist George Gamow

an answer to the question he had been asking himself: How did the first and simplest elements in the universe (hydrogen and helium) come into existence? Since an expanding universe must have started from smaller beginnings, he suggested that the simple elements were synthesized long before the formation of the stars in an incredibly hot, compact furnace of neutron gas. This, he said, was the starting point of Hubble's expanding universe.

Gamow, a brilliant scientist who found detail tedious, wanted to know what temperature space should be today after the cooling of such a fireball containing all the matter in the universe. He gave the job of figuring this out to 2 colleagues, Alpher and Herman. These 2 workers made the detailed calculations necessary to predict that today's space, 15 billion years after the Big Bang, should be filled with microwave radiation at a temperature of 5°C above absolute zero (5°K) with a characteristic radiation spectrum for that temperature.

In 1965, the predicted microwave radiation was indeed detected by Penzias and Wilson, indicating that the temperature of space was 3.5°K, close to Alpher and Herman's forecast. Penzias and Wilson had won the cigar or, in this case, a Nobel prize for supplying the best evidence yet in support of Gamow's Big Bang theory of the creation or matter.

Fred Hoyle, a nuclear physicist knighted in England for his contributions to science, buys none of this. "All wrong," says Sir Fred who refuses to believe that the universe could be created by a big bang from nothing.

In 1946, Hoyle and 2 physicist friends Bondi and Gold saw a movie that, according to Hoyle, had a circular plot whose end matched the beginning. After the movie, it is said that the 3 gathered around a case of Bondi's rum and, stimulated by the intoxicating fluid, formulated what has come to be known as the Steady State theory.

The Steady State universe expands forever and everywhere looks the same. There is no starting point and there is no end. Galaxies are created continuously from the spontaneous generation of new matter, and they fill the spaces left by the galaxies that are receding.

Of these 2 conflicting views of the universe, Gamow's Big Bang theory has effectively won out over Hoyle's Steady State concept. Discoveries since 1964 have hammered one coffin nail after another into the Hoyle hypothesis. For example, Hoyle's continuous creation scenario does not predict any left over cosmic background radiation from a primeval fireball. However, this radiation was discovered by Penzias and Wilson in 1964-65. Another coffin nail: according to the Steady State theory, the unchanging universe should look the same everywhere. It does not. The early universe, as detected by radiation from the most distant galaxies, contains objects such as quasars that are absent in the later, nearer universe.

By the late 1970's most of the original Steady-Staters (excepting Sir Fred) had quietly retired into the woodwork, saying little more about their theory. It is ironic that the name Big Bang was given by Hoyle himself to the concept of creation that he so persistently opposed. The name stuck like glue and was happily adopted by the very supporters of the theory whom, perhaps, it was intended to discredit.

The Big Bang concept, as it stands today, may be explained in these general terms.

About 15 billion years ago, all the matter and energy that we can detect in the universe, including galaxies with their trillions of stars, was crammed into a space smaller than your finger nail. This concentrated mass of charged particles and radiation, incomprehensible to the human mind, had a temperature and density considered to be infinitely high. When, in the mother of all explosions, it blew apart, it did so by a process called inflation (nothing to do with depreciating money) where, for the tiniest fraction of a second ($10^{-32}$ sec), gravity reversed its role and acted to repel instead of attract. It is hardly surprising that the laws of nature under such incredibly hot, dense conditions acted in strange ways.

After 300,000 years of blistering expansion, inflation was replaced by normal physics as protons and electrons combined to form hydrogen atoms and then added neutrons to make helium. Slight regional variations in the density of this expanding soup led to the clumping of hydrogen and helium which, after a billion years, commenced to seed the universe with galaxies of young stars in enormous sheets and filaments.

Some critics maintain that ordinary matter like hydrogen and helium could not exert enough gravitational pull to clump in this way. To account for galaxy formation, they propose that 99 percent of matter in the universe is 'cold dark matter' made of particles other than protons, neutrons, and electrons, that have enough gravitational pull to start the clumping process. This added matter, as a bonus, would give the necessary mass to halt an otherwise unending expansion of the universe. The problem with the cold dark matter idea is that none has ever been detected.

**QUASARS**

'Quasar' was once the brand name of a popular TV set. The word seems to have a modern, high-tech ring. In that sense, it is a misnomer. High-tech perhaps, but quasars are anything but modern. Those whose light we can see today were born many billions of years ago. Since the time their light began its journey from there to here, they have probably winked out.

What exactly is a quasar? It is thought to be the brilliant radiation produced by matter falling into a black hole. The radiation may exceed that of a hundred billion suns coming from a space perhaps no bigger than our solar system. It is because it is so powerful that we can see such a small object from as far as 15 billion light years away.

How do quasars work? Where are they located?

In the center of galaxies, one or more black holes are believed to exist, created when a large star (bigger than our sun) runs out of fuel and collapses under its own weight. It theoretically contracts to pin-point size with gravity so great that light cannot escape. When other stars come near it, they are ripped apart, swallowed, and similarly compacted. After a hundred million or so stars have been grabbed and mistreated like this, the black hole has built up enough gravity to attract surrounding cosmic gas from light years away. The heat and radiation generated by the infalling gas light up space with the most powerful brilliance in the universe. This is a quasar.

Having pulled off an unparalleled display of fireworks, what does the quasar do next? It simply peters out. After 50 million years or so, when the gas and dust in its vicinity is swept clean, the quasar is out of fuel and 'switches off'. It then reverts to its former unseen existence as an anonymous black hole. If a hapless star wanders close, it is captured into small, rapid orbits that end with a bright flare as the star is torn up and digested. The center of the galaxy is eventually vacuumed clean of its star-forming gas by the black hole.

Quasars peaked in number 2 to 3 billion years after the Big Bang. Today they are seen with a frequency of one quasar per 100,000 galaxies. Some quasar activity may have occurred as an early, brief stage in the formation of all galaxies including the Milky Way. The ones we can still see are so far away that they allow us to look back nearer to the apparent beginning of time.

## BUBBLE UNIVERSES

Human beings will, no doubt, keep inventing theories about the creation of the universe until they get it right. Robert Dicke, working with James Peebles at Princeton University in the 1960's, extended Gamow's Big Bang concept to include a universe that cycled between big bangs and big crunches. It was Dicke, incidentally, who alerted Penzias and Wilson in 1964-65 that the 'noise' from their microwave antenna was the afterglow of the last big bang. Inevitably, perhaps, Dicke's cycling concept was followed by the grander-scale speculations of physicists like Allen Guth and Andrei Linde, pioneers of an inflationary cosmos based on the energy of 'scalar fields'.

Linde's grand scheme is of 'many inflating balls that produce new balls, which in turn produce more balls, ad infinitum.' He calls this 'an eternally existing, self-reproducing, inflationary universe.' According to Linde, our own ball (the universe we live in) has become so large that we see only a small part of it. Inflation, Linde believes, may have caused this ball to expand, in much less than a second, from a size smaller than one centimeter ($10^{-33}$cm) to a size equal to $10^{1,000,000,000,000}$ centimeters. To grasp this stupefying increase, note that the universe we see around us with our most powerful instruments is, by comparison, a very small $10^{28}$ centimeters in size.

The universe is not restricted, Linde believes, to our own bubble. Ours is only one of an infinite number, each sprouting off new buds in an unending, chain-like reaction. In Linde's words, "Each particular part of the universe (such as our bubble) may stem from a singularity (point of infinite density and temperature) somewhere in the past and it may end up in a singularity somewhere in the future. There is, however, no end for the evolution of the entire universe." Linde postulates physical laws and space/time dimensions in other bubbles quite different from our own, and thinks that we find ourselves in our bubble simply because it may not be possible for our kind or life to exist in others.

## CLOSER TO HOME

For personal, practical purposes, the other bubbles of an extended universe (if they exist) would seem to have little significance for us. Unless we discover wormhole travel, and learn to tolerate alien physical laws and dimensions, we will not be vacationing in other bubble domains (except perhaps after death).

The prospect of remote travel in our own visible universe, although tantalizing, obviously involves insurmountable distances. The nearest galaxy to us, Andromeda, although only a stone's throw away, would take 2 million years to reach traveling at the impossible speed of light. Unless there are unforeseen technical breakthroughs, we are destined to journey, at best, within our own galaxy.

We live in one of the spiral arms of the Milky Way galaxy, about

30,000 light years from its center. Our nearest star neighbor is Alpha Centauri, 4 light years away. If we journeyed there, we might, or might not, find planets. Stars burn so brightly that their light blinds us to the possible presence of orbiting planets.

There is certainly a large choice of stars to visit in the Milky Way, if we could get to them. About 100 billion stars. It would take 3,000 years, counting one per second, just to tally this number. These stars, like our sun, were condensed from a cloud of hydrogen and helium atoms which were forged during the hot, dense, initial stages of the Big Bang. The ratio of radioactive isotopes in meteorites that have fallen to earth from space suggest that star formation in our galaxy commenced some 15 to 17 billion years ago. Most of the primordial gas that once existed near the center has coalesced into stars, fallen into a black hole, or been expelled by exploding supernova debris.

Eventually, all stars in our bubble universe will exhaust their fuel and the Milky Way, like other galaxies, will blink out, leaving behind a population of white dwarfs and black holes. Unless, of course, our bubble contains enough mass to start contracting, in which case the big chill will become a big, infinitely hot crunch. Stay tuned.

## PART II. THE ARRIVAL OF LIFE

### EARLY EARTH

The event that set our own personal futures on course was the birth, 4.6 billion years ago, of the solar system. The objects in this microscopic region of the cosmos condensed by accretion from a cloud of primeval hydrogen and helium gas, mixed with heavier elements bequeathed (tax free) by old supernova explosions. Our sun (100 times the diameter of Earth) had enough gravity to turn itself into a nuclear fireball. Its 9 orbiting planets, too small to make nuclear fireworks on their own, passively absorb and reflect the sun's stupendous radiation.

Little Earth, from the standpoint of human history, was fortunately placed at the proper distance from the sun to avoid being fried or frozen. And yet, for the first half billion years or so, its terrain was predictably turbulent. Looking at the moon's cratered surface, we can immediately understand this. Large asteroids and meteors rained down from space creating hell on earth with each collision. If this weren't enough, the planet's hot interior erupted through volcanic fissures to layer vast plains with molten rock. Eventually, outgassing from the mantle produced both an atmosphere (mostly carbon dioxide and nitrogen) and voluminous quantities of water which became the oceans. The shifting crust, erosion, and mountain formation reworked the bare surface until it no longer looked like the pock-marked face of the moon.

And what do you know? Life appeared.

## MYSTERIOUS START

Not on 4 legs, of course. The earliest clues we have are the imprints recently obtained in sediment in northwestern Australia made by microbes resembling blue-green algae, called cyanobacteria. The rock from which these filamentous, beaded fossils were found is calculated by radioactive dating to be 3.465 billion years old. Space debris stopped its hellish bombardment of the Earth's surface about 3.9 billion years ago, so life had a period of, say, 400 million years to be created and to develop to the stage of this relatively simple organism.

Did life arise only once, or were there false starts? Did it begin in one place, or many? Since no earlier fossils have been found, we have to guess the answers to these questions.

Perhaps the first question to attempt is *how* life got started on Earth. People once thought that beetles and other smallish living things arose spontaneously from soil or dirt. Louis Pasteur showed that this was not so, demonstrating that they all had living *parents*. It is now generally believed that all today's life is related to those early cyanobacteria that lived 3.5 billion years ago.

But those bacteria, although single-celled and lacking a cell nucleus, were surely far too complex to arise spontaneously from inanimate material. Pasteur would ask: What were the *first* living organisms?

We think of soup as a nutritious liquid that warms us up on a wintry day. The term 'primordial soup' is what geologists sometimes call the warm, watery solution believed to have covered much of the Earth's rocky surface about a billion years after the solar system was formed. Biologists guess that the primordial soup gave birth to the earliest forms of life, suggesting that they arose at random from simple carbon compounds in the soup that combined to form more complex biological molecules. These molecules, inanimate by themselves, united to form living organisms which could replicate themselves. By analogy, it is said that a monkey, if left at a typewriter long enough, would ultimately type out the complete works of Shakespeare by sheer chance. The Precambrian seas, bathed in the energy of sunlight, erupting volcanoes, and violent electrical storms had plenty of time, like the monkey, to put together a living molecular unit also by chance.

Scientists like to analyze nature in the lab. Stanley Miller was no exception. He tried to mimic prelife conditions on the early planet by mixing heated water and its vapor with methane, ammonia, and hydrogen gases through which he sent high voltage sparks such as those that could result from lightning strikes. Miller created no life in his mixture, but after a week of experimentation he did recover organic chemicals, including amino acids (the building blocks of life).

Even if life was synthesized in the seas by random processes, possibly near geothermal vents in the sea floor or in the sunbaked surface foam, we are still left with the problem: how did it replicate? Was a DNA molecule mysteriously formed in the primordial soup that could somehow make the enzymes required for its own replication? This would be a tall order. Some investigators think it more likely that undiscovered reactions in the prebiotic ocean could have led to the synthesis of RNA-type molecules that had a capacity to replicate by acting as their own catalysts without the help of proteins.

Not all scientists, by any means, have bought into the hypothesis of spontaneous life from the random aggregation of simpler molecules.

We know from spectral observation of interstellar space that there are organic molecules out there. For example, in May 1994, the amino acid glycine was found in the star-forming cloud near the center of our galaxy, Sagittarius B 2. Some scientists believe such organic compounds were brought to earth by those same comets, asteroids, and meteors that were making early life so hazardous. The remains of fallen meteorites indeed contain organic compounds, including adenine and guanine (constituents of RNA and DNA) and amino acids. Those that survived the intense heat of arrival may have contributed to life's origin on earth.

Fred Hoyle, always the contrary thinker, believes that earthly life was indeed seeded from space. He has reportedly said that spontaneous generation of life on earth would have been as likely as the assemblage of a 747 aircraft by a tornado passing through a junkyard. This prestigious astrophysicist is further convinced that space is teeming with microbes, a view that is hardly shared by most scientists.

## A UNICELLULAR WORLD

Once life got started on Earth, a strange thing happened. It stayed the same, that is, unicellular, for almost 3 billion years. The first half of this 3 billion year period saw unicellular organisms without a nucleus (prokaryote). In the second half, the cell nucleus was invented (eukaryote) and this enclosed the cell's DNA. The second half also coincided with the creation of an oxygen atmosphere, thanks probably to the photo synthetic activity of the globe's unicellular population.

And then, suddenly, after 3 billion years, there was a radical change. Multicellular (many-celled) organisms came into existence and rapidly increased in numbers. This remarkable event occurred over the short geological time span of 5 million years. Biologist and historian Stephen Jay Gould comments about this:

'3 billion years of unicellularity followed by 5 million years of intense creativity and then capped by more than 500 million years of variation on set anatomical themes can scarcely be read as a predictable, inexorable or continuous trend toward progress or increasing complexity.... The most salient feature of life has been the stability of its bacterial mode.... The number of E. Coli cells in the gut of each human being exceeds the number of human beings that have ever lived on this planet.... (Scientific American, Oct. 1994).'

In other words, in the history of life, the more things change, the more they stay the same.

## CHANGING LIFE FORMS

When 2 humans give birth to a child, the new baby will be human like its parents. Similarly, when a hen lays an egg, the farmer would be surprised, indeed, to see a lobster or a tulip hatch out instead of a chick. A species is expected to breed true. The general characteristics that are found in the offspring will normally be those that were present in the parents.

But this principle of species constancy has actually not prevailed during the latter part of Earth's history. As anyone can see, there has been an explosion of species on the planet ranging in variety from the dandelion to the dinosaur, neither of which even vaguely resembles the very early life forms. Even today, some species are becoming extinct while others are arising. What is going on here? Why did not all life stay the way it originally was?

## FROM MICROBE TO MAN

The extraordinary diversity of life on Earth, consisting of many millions of bacteria, plant, and animal species, remained a mystery until recently. How did all those different shapes, structures, and functional differences arise? 2 centuries ago, the common belief was that all species were created as we find them today and that they remain that way.

Charles Darwin thought differently. He proposed that all of the world's species evolved from a few primitive predecessors, and developed into their present forms through a process he called 'natural selection'. Another naturalist, Arthur Wallace, who lived in Darwin's time, had similar ideas, but he lacked the detailed evidence presented by Darwin that eventually convinced the world that the theory is right. Many people today, including most scientists, no longer believe in the *literal* Biblical account of divine creation. This is largely due to Darwin's work and insight.

Darwin was an extremely methodical and painstaking researcher who spent years on a shipboard expedition examining different species of organism in their natural habitats. Indifferent to seasickness and tropical disease, he gathered an astonishing amount of data to support his theory of evolution which was published in 1859 in the book: *The Origin of Species.*

The essence of Darwin's work is this: he observed that new traits occurring apparently at random in a species sometimes enable the species to cope with changes in the environment that might otherwise be lethal. He postulated that a single organism with such a beneficial change passes it on to its young which then multiply and flourish in the hostile or altered environment. In this way, an old species dies out and is superseded by a new, better adapted species through the process unsentimentally referred to as natural selection or *survival of the fittest.* If the kitchen gets too hot, you can stay there only if you acquire a new trait that makes you immune to the heat.

But how are these new traits acquired? The nineteenth century French naturalist Lamarck thought that giraffes got long necks by stretching them to reach for food, then passed on this *acquired* condition to their offspring. Darwin did not believe in the inheritance of *acquired* traits.

## MUTATIONS FOR DIVERSITY

Darwin didn't know why some offspring had different traits than those appearing in their family tree. The mechanism, which he called 'hereditary variability', was obscure to him. He just observed that it happened, and went on from there.

If new traits don't come about by changing habits, as in neck stretching, then how are they produced? The answer lies in the DNA molecule. We will talk about this remarkable entity after we have looked at some historic landmarks in the study of heredity. This will ultimately leave us staring at DNA and the mutations that produce new traits and diversity.

The initial breakthrough in understanding heredity was made in the nineteenth century when a religious monk and teacher named Gregor Mendel meticulously crossbred sweetpeas in his monastery garden at Saint Thomas in Austria. His private experiments led him to discover the classical rules governing the inheritance of dominant and recessive traits in plants. Knowing the parents, he was able to predict the characteristics of the offspring.

Mendel lived in Darwin's time, but his work did not receive recognition until both men were dead. The rules that Mendel formulated, as important as they were, did not shed any light on the physical mechanism for heredity, that is, *how* the organism passed on its traits.

This insight came half a century later when Thomas Hunt Morgan found that the thread-like objects called chromosomes in the nuclei of germ cells (the cells that form the young) are the key to the puzzle of heredity. These chromosomes carried the 'genes', or heritable units, responsible for the inheritance of traits observed by Mendel, and he established that the genes are arranged in linear order on the chromosomes. With Morgan's discovery of genes on chromosomes, the science of genetics was blossoming.

Another breakthrough came from the work of De Vries, a contemporary of Morgan. De Vries noted that the genes on chromosomes were subject to random *mutations*, or changes, which could give rise to new traits in the offspring. In other words, the appearance of new traits which Darwin had observed but could not explain were now traced to random changes on chromosomes. Darwin identified the changes in species and noticed how they affected the survival of the species. De Vries linked these changes to random alterations on the chromosomes.

The icing on the cake was provided by James Watson and Francis Crick who collaborated in 1953 to achieve one of the most stunning scientific breakthroughs of all time. They discovered the precise molecular structure of DNA, the molecule in chromosomes responsible for inherited traits.

Watson and Crick were in a desperate race with Nobel laureate Linus Pauling for this discovery which they felt sure would reveal the mechanism of heredity. The race was close, but Watson and Crick won by a head. For their brilliant work they took home a Nobel prize. The 'molecule of life' stood naked, and the world could examine its intricate details. Watson and Crick had made it possible, at last, for scientists to see exactly how mutations work. The mystery of Darwin's 'hereditary variability' could now be explored and explained at a molecular level. The complex clock had been taken apart and the need for guesswork concerning the diversity of life on the planet was disappearing.

## HOW MUTATIONS WORK

Today's elephant has little in common with the single-celled ancestor that preceded it by three and a half billion years. One can hardly believe there is a connection between the 2 organisms, yet a connection exists. The elephant actually arose directly from its ancient, primitive predecessor through billions of intervening generations, all of which were subject to mutations. These mutations, each hardly noticeable in itself, nevertheless added up over time to produce the dramatic differences in the size, shape, and function seen between the elephant and the microbe.

When we say mutations, we mean changes in DNA, life's diminutive template. Since DNA is the printing press, as it were, that stamps out proteins, and because proteins are the building blocks of the body and the catalysts of its chemical factories, we can see that changes in the DNA will cause changes in the body's construction and function.

To understand this, let's walk into the cell nucleus, take out our magnifying glass, and scrutinize the DNA that is located there. As we focus on the first DNA molecule that comes into view, we notice that it consists of 2 very long strands wound around each other to form the famous DNA helix first revealed by Watson and Crick in 1953. Each strand is largely composed of *nucleotide* molecules, and it is this nucleotide part that we wish to focus on here.

There are 4 different kinds of nucleotide present in each DNA strand, abbreviated by the letters A, C, G, and T. From our position standing in the nucleus, we can see that these nucleotides A, C, G, and T are strung along the whole enormous length of each of the 2 intertwined DNA strands. Now, it is the *order* in which these 4 different nucleotides are sequenced that tells the cell what kind of protein to make. Each protein has its own special nucleotide sequence on a small segment of the DNA strand that codes for it alone and not for any other type of protein. Since there is a nucleotide sequence for every protein, and since proteins determine body traits, it is easy to see that body traits depend on the order of nucleotides along the DNA molecule. The more complex the organism, the greater the number of proteins and therefore the more nucleotide sequences and DNA the organism will have.

Anything that can change one or more of the 4 types of nucleotide by removal, damage, or replacement will, of course, change the nucleotide sequence. Because of this change, or mutation, of the nucleotide sequence, the protein corresponding to that sequence will also be changed.

If only one cell gets mutated, it won't matter, because there are countless other cells that remain unmutated and will produce the normal protein as before. But hold on. Suppose the cell in which this mutation occurs is a *germ* cell, let's say an egg cell in the ovary, then what happens? In such a case, the new individual arising from the union of that egg cell with a sperm cell will carry the mutation in all its cells. The original cell will divide many times to form an adult, and because DNA copies itself exactly at each division, mutation and all, the adult will end up with every cell in its body a mutated cell making altered protein. This change to the protein made by DNA may be a critical one, and show up as an altered body trait. This is the way Darwin's 'hereditary variability' is linked to mutations.

## KICK YOUR RADIO AND MAKE IT WORK

Although some mutations give rise to vitally important traits and help a species survive, not all mutations are helpful. In fact, most mutations are harmful. Random destructive changes to DNA would hardly be expected to produce a useful change in an organism. We know from experience that, if we poke around in a careless way with any delicate piece of equipment, we are likely to do more harm than good. But occasionally, you can kick your radio and make it work! In the same way, with the trillions of mutations constantly occurring in a species, a small percentage of these changes will be useful, and adapt the mutated members of the species to demanding changes in the environment.

A good example is seen when most disease-causing bacteria are wiped out by an anti-biotic drug such as penicillin. Some of these bugs undergo mutations that happen to make them resistant to the lethal effects of the drug. These resistant microbes then flourish, multiply, and continue to make the patient sick. This is unfortunate for the patient, but fortunate for the bugs.

## HIT BY AN INCOMING MISSILE

Our talk about mutations has so far focused on how they are inherited, and what effect they have on the parent and offspring. It seems fair, now, to ask: what causes a mutation to occur in the first place? What would make a nucleotide or nucleotide sequence in DNA change, thereby causing a mutation? If you were a self-respecting nucleotide in a DNA molecule, why would you want to change?

Well, you might be obliged to change if an incoming particle of radiation hit you, bang! where it hurts, knocking an electron out of your structure. Such an event would make you, the nucleotide, extremely reactive chemically and likely to change from the nucleotide you were into something else. Such a hit from an incoming missile would alter the normal sequence of nucleotides in the DNA molecule and the protein it makes. This alteration could be harmful or helpful.

Harmful damage to nucleotide sequences often happens to us when we are exposed to ionizing radiation. 'Ionizing' is the kind that knocks electrons out of atoms. Such radiation can arrive from the sun, cosmic space, or radioactive minerals in the ground. For example, skin cancer is on the increase because the ozone layer of the upper atmosphere is thinning out, letting in more of the sun's destructive ultraviolet rays. We get skin cancer from this. The rays cause the cells in our skin to mutate, turning them into cancer cells. Similarly, radon gas seeping up through cracks in your basement can reach your lungs, changing the normal cells into malignant cells.

The worst sort of radiation is usually made by mankind. We are all familiar with them: medical X-rays, radioactive dumps, thermonuclear explosions, atomic powerplant meltdowns. The cancers produced by the Chernobyl catastrophe in the former USSR is testimony to the havoc that radiation can produce when man lets his genie out of the bottle. The cancers produced by the atomic bomb blasts over Hiroshima and Nagasaki are no less discouraging.

Radiation isn't the only threat to our DNA. Our nucleotides can be damaged by other means. How often do we hear of some company, institution, or government getting sued for putting cancer-causing products in the food, air, or ground? These materials can react with the nucleotides in the DNA of our cells, causing them to mutate into cancer cells.

If we manage to avoid such threatening materials, we are still not in the clear. Nucleotide sequences, besides being altered by radiation and chemicals, can also be changed by errors of DNA replication at the time of cell division. It is easy for the cell to make a mistake at this time, and quite extraordinary that more errors don't happen considering the trillions of cell divisions that occur in the human body over a lifetime. When the cell divides, each DNA molecule is expected to make an exact copy of itself even though it contains hundreds of thousands of nucleotides. The chances for total accuracy at every division are not good. It is fortunate for us that our DNA is often able to repair its own mutations because, as noted, most are harmful. Indeed, when causing cancer, often lethal.

**ENGINEERED EVOLUTION**

The evolution of life has proceeded on Earth without human intervention and, for billions of years, without mankind's presence. This is probably about to change. Now that we have learned how to transplant individual genes (segments of DNA), we will use this technique more and more for treating heritable diseases. We have already succeeded putting DNA into microorganisms for the manufacture of useful products in previously unheard of quantities. We will soon find other ways to manipulate DNA that will be of great benefit to mankind.

Marvin Minsky, a pioneer in artificial intelligence and robotics, sees another change coming in the way humans influence their own evolution. He notes that impulses travel in the human brain at a snail's pace when compared to the speed of a computer. Minsky visualizes a future application of advanced computers as direct attachments, via microscopic electrodes, to the brain. Such electronic assists, he speculates, could enormously increase the speed at which the brain processes certain kinds of information, and greatly enhance our ability to learn. He also believes humans will invent electronic creatures with brains that employ the same parallel thinking circuits used by humans but capable of greater speed. As Minsky phrases it:

'The events in our computer chips already happen millions of times faster than those in brain cells. Hence, we could design our 'mind children' to think a million times faster than we do. To such a being, half a minute might seem as long as one of our years and each hour as long as an entire human lifetime ...' . (Scientific American, Oct. 1994)

Another speculator about sense of time and speed of thought is mathematical physicist Frank Tipler, author of The Physics of Immortality. Tipler thinks that the universe someday will contract back to an 'Omega' point. The Library of Science interprets his view this way:

'In the last minutes of existence, all information from past ages will converge into a light cone centered on ... vast intelligences. The information will include the past-life history of every living being that ever existed, including all humans. The superbeings will be able to simulate the life of every human in those last minutes, so that each of us will essentially be "resurrected" by the infinitely powerful superbeings, which assume the role of God ... . Time can be measured by *the number of thoughts processed,* rather than by the ticks on some clock. The infinitely fast workings of the God-like superbeing will ensure an eternity of time in which our emulated selves can exist.'

This is the way, according to Tipler, that humans derive their immortality. Like Zeno's paradox of infinite incremental steps, the end never comes.

## PURPOSE

Is anybody at the controls in this universe, or are we on random automatic? Is there some purpose, intent, or plan behind our world? Opinions are not hard to come by.

The theologian tells us: "Matters of purpose are not for humans to comprehend. Believe in God, do what he asks, and all bases will be covered in this world and the next."

The Agnostic rejoins: "Which God? No God has been rationally revealed. Forget about purpose. The hereafter? Pie in the sky!"

The Scientist, who is out looking under rocks to see what he can turn up for analysis, says: "Purpose is a *why* question. I don't ask why, I ask how." He hopes to put together a unified *how* theory-of-everything.

The Saved Memory Hypothesis advocate, like the others, has

no illuminating ideas about purpose. "In the absence of evidence," he says, "we can only guess by using our intuition." He cautions against blind acceptance of dogma.

Men and women are learning more about the world they live in with every daily advance of science. They may soon be aided by genetically or electronically engineered changes to their brain. Ultimately, they may even receive helpful information from civilizations in other worlds. As information accumulates, hypotheses that are not testable now (such as the Saved Memory Hypothesis) may become testable. On the other hand, if Fred Hoyle is right and we blow ourselves up, it will be the lot of some other organism to evolve and do the testing.

# APPENDIX I

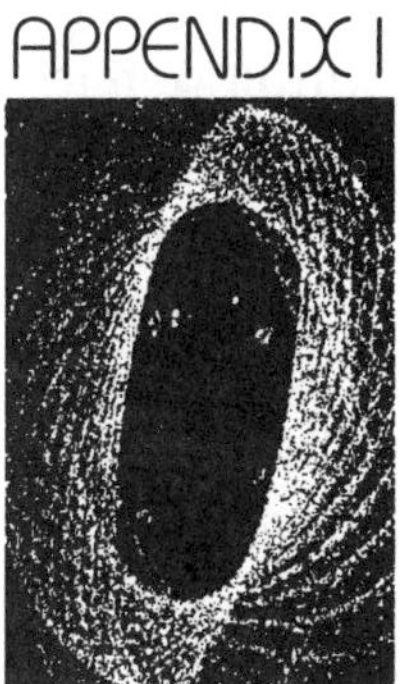

Although *new* traits arise spontaneously in a species by mutation, *existing* traits are passed from parents to offspring in new combinations that do not involve mutation. The diverse parental traits form a mix in the fertilized egg that produces an individual different from either parent. Thus, Mary may get her Mom's blue eyes and blond hair, but inherit her Dad's long legs and freckles. The mix is brought about by processes known as random assortment and crossover of chromosomes.

1. In fertilized eggs, chromosomes (and therefore genes) come in pairs, one from the father and one from the mother. Each member, or allele, of the pair is different in the effect it can produce which, as Mendel noted, may be 'dominant' or 'recessive' in character. A dominant 'allele' (D), for example, might produce a trait such as the production of pigment, whereas its recessive allele (d) might produce none. If the allele combination in the fertilized cell should be (DD) or (Dd), pigment would be produced; if (dd), it would not. There are many germ cells, each carrying one of these alleles, which could combine at fertilization. Which alleles actually do end up together as a pair in the fertilized cell is a chance event, and hence the process is referred to as 'random assortment' of genes.

2. The randomness of allele recombination in the fertilized egg is increased by another process called 'crossover'. This occurs in the parent germ cell during meiotic division when paired chromosomes lie side by side and exchange segments of DNA

and the genes which are located on those segments. It is as if ten red-coated soldiers forming part of a long line were to change places with ten blue-coated soldiers opposite them in another long line. When these chromosomes separate at cell division, they will contain interchanged segments, thus increasing their diversity.

The overall result of random assortment and crossover of chromosomes is to provide a greater variety of trait combinations in an organism's offspring, and hence improve the species' chances of successfully meeting new challenges in a changing environment. Johnny might succumb, but his brother Jim, endowed with a more suitable combination of traits, might flourish and breed.

# APPENDIX II: CELL ENERGY

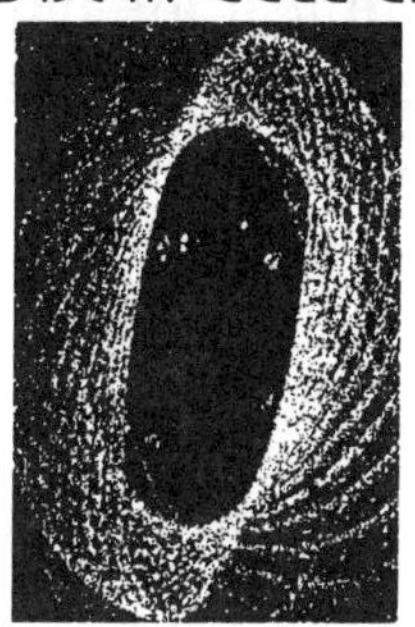

The form of energy that is used best by animal cells comes from a molecule known as ATP which is made in the cell by a process, as has already been noted, called oxidative phosphorylation. In this process the food, let's say glucose sugar, is dismantled chemically in the cell, and this dismantling causes the sugar to lose some energy which, it turns out, the cell cannot use directly for its work. However, the cell is able instead to take the energy released by the sugar and use it to upgrade a relatively low energy molecule called ADP into the higher energy molecule ATP. The cell can draw upon this energy reserve at will for its many needs by breaking down ATP again to ADP. The reaction is reversible. This conversion back and forth between ATP and ADP with the transfer and release of energy is going on continually inside the cell. The released energy is used by the cell to power the incredible number and variety of chemical reactions involved in its daily work. The cell may not have a brain, but its manipulations, such as obtaining energy from sugar, proceed flawlessly, are self directed, and go on twenty-four hours a day.

The conversion of ADP to ATP by phosphorylation occurs in the interior of cell organelles called mitochondria, and requires oxygen which is obtained by diffusion into the cell. The phosphorylation reaction also requires the participation of fifty or more enzymes, made from protein, which must be positioned relative to one another in a very exact spatial sequence for the reaction to occur. Evidence shows that these enzymes are lined up in the appropriate order within and upon infoldings of the mitochondrial membrane. It is here that the high energy ATP molecules are formed, and from here that they travel out of the mitochondrion to reach the rest of the cell.

# APPENDIX III: MAKING PROTEIN

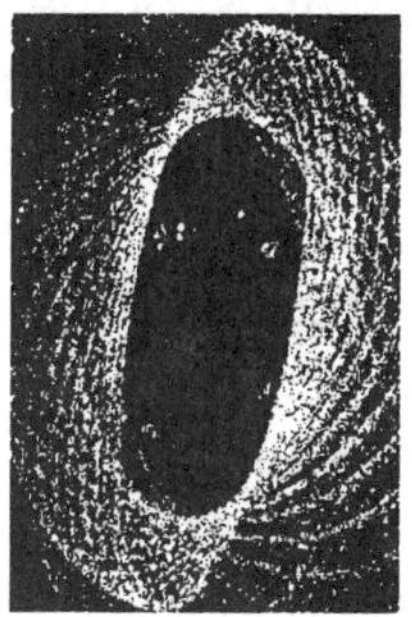

Watson and Crick opened the window through which it is possible to observe the incredible achievement of the cell in organizing the gala dance of amino acids as they lock arms to form the proteins of life. Thc basic maneuvers of the dance are mechanical and straight forward. That is what Arthur Murray taught in his one, two, three-step diagrams. Get from A to B in the right order, don't trip up, and always follow instructions. The Arthur Murray motto is also the plan of action followed by amino acid molecules as they construct proteins. Let's see if we can trace some of their dance steps.

It all begins, as you could guess, with the DNA molecule as it sits in the nucleus of the cell. Human DNA carries the code for making all the different proteins of the body. This code will soon be deciphered by the impressive scientific undertaking called the Human Genome Project that aims to identify the building instructions for every protein in the human cell.

Our first step in following the cha-cha-cha that constructs proteins is to recognize how the dancing instructions are printed on the DNA molecule so that they may be conveyed to the amino acid molecules waiting in the wings. The DNA molecule, you may remember, is composed of two very long threads, each containing nucleotide units A, T, C, and G attached in series like links in a chain. Now, here comes a critical point in our story: each of the twenty amino acids in the cell recognizes one particular sequence of three nucleotides, called a codon. When an amino acid sees these special nucleotides in a row, it is permitted to shout: "Hey, that codon is for me, and only for me!" Unfortunately for the simplicity of our account, another issue must be introduced. The amino acids are in the cytoplasm outside the nucleus and so do not have direct contact with DNA which is contained within the nucleus in the nucleoplasm. How, then, can the amino acids outside find out about the nucleotide sequences on the DNA molecules inside? DNA itself provides the solution to this problem. It sends a messenger out of the nucleus among the amino acids, and this messenger carries the same pattern of nucleotide sequences that are inscribed on the DNA. This messenger molecule is called messenger RNA, or m-RNA for short.

The nucleotide sequence for one single protein takes up only a short segment of a DNA chain. Let's imagine a protein that is made up of a string of one hundred amino acids. Since each amino acid recognizes a special sequence of three nucleotides, in order to make the protein we would need a DNA strand of three hundred nucleotides in correct sequence to carry the code for our protein. What happens is this: DNA unwinds its two strands to lay bare the three hundred nucleotides, then copies that sequence in the form of an m-RNA messenger molecule. This m-RNA copy leaves the nucleus to find the amino acids in the cytoplasm outside the nucleus.

Now, further complications. We would like to introduce you to another cell organelle called the ribosome. These small, dense bodies populate the cell cytoplasm in numbers almost too large to count. What do these organelles do to earn their keep? They are central to our amino acid dance, for it is on ribosomes that protein molecules are constructed from amino acids. Also, it is to the ribosomes that m-RNA messenger molecules, with their special nucleotide sequences, become attached after they leave the nucleus.

Let's summarize:

1. DNA in the nucleus carries the code for constructing all of the proteins made in the cell;

2. DNA duplicates this code in short segments called m-RNA molecules;

3. m-RNA molecules leave the nucleus and attach themselves to the ribosome organelles in the cytoplasm of the cell.

What happens now? Where do we go next in the dance of the amino acids? We will focus our attention on a final complication to our story. This complication takes the form of a molecule called transfer RNA, or t-RNA. These t-RNA molecules, swimming freely in the cytoplasm with the amino acids, can be thought of as having two ends: one end wants to hold hands with one particular kind of amino acid, whereas the other end is only interested in linking up with a particular codon, or nucleotide sequence, on the m-RNA molecule. These attachments do, indeed, occur. First, the t-RNA finds and attaches to its favorite amino acid with one end, then the t-RNA/amino acid combination locks by its other end to its matching codon on the m-RNA thread. The ribosome (remember it?) acts as a policeman directing traffic, seeing to it that the t-RNA/amino acid groups are added in line, one at a time like letters to a word, along the length of the m-RNA thread. As the t-RNA/amino acid groups are lined up in this fashion, each amino acid grabs its neighbor's hand in a daisy chain. The chain, on reaching the right length with the correct number of amino acid molecules, is released from the m-RNA thread as a bona fide protein. This ingenious amino acid dance, with all its intricate steps, continues unabated throughout the life of the cell. The music stops when cell death occurs, bringing a halt to the antics of the whirling dancers.

# EPILOGUE

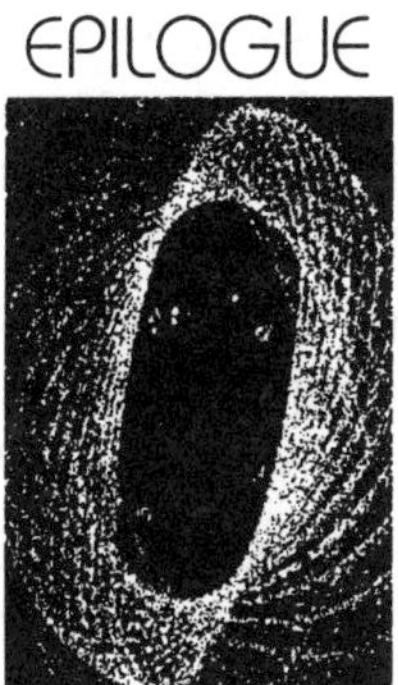

A respected scientist read this manuscript before the galley proofs were released to the Publisher. He complained: "Hey, you left me hanging — you didn't tie everything together at the end."

Hence this epilogue.

The Reader and the Author have taken a voyage, not in a real ship as Darwin did, but by means of our minds. Has this mental exercise brought to light any new insights concerning our existence? Is it author arrogance to suppose that some of the ideas presented here might have nudged the Reader's thinking into unexplored channels?

Our winding and tortuous voyage has touched at many ports of call. In this short epilogue, the Author invites the Reader to accompany him in a Brief review of some of the principal sites that have been visited, looking at them from the perspective of the Saved Memory Hypothesis.

The first major port of call is the Saved Memory Hypothesis itself. This alleges that the entire panorama of Earthly life may be preserved in a post mortem existence exactly as it was originally sensed. The Hypothesis, with many elaborations, is the thread that persistently runs through *Surviving Death*. The *impermanence* of mortal life, and the transitory nature of the physical objects around us, is highlighted at this port of call by images of rotting corpses, exploding worlds, and crunching universes. We are shown that the Self escapes this cauldron of instability by the *continuous* transfer of the memorized events of our lives to an indestructible milieu where subjective consciousness reappears and a new 'life' begins.

The next major port of call in the book is the Self. In any hypothesis of life after death, the Self is paramount, for this is what could survive. Our extended visit at this port gives us a picture of Self as a composite, formed from our ongoing sensory input that is hard-wired in a physical memory and accessed by consciousness. It is made clear at this port of call that a relocated, reanimated, post mortem memory makes the death of our body an irrelevant event. In effect, the material world may be blown away, but every atom of its ordered structure is preserved in the immortal memories of those who were there. The world and the Self, in this sense, are indestructible.

Another important port of call in *Surviving Death* is *religion.* We see here a multitude of contrasting views concerning life after death. The Saved Memory Hypothesis also has its own distinct postulates in this regard. We note, however, that there is one idea common to all the major religions and the Saved Memory Hypothesis. It is that human behaviour in this life will influence the quality of existence in the next.

After a provocative stay at Religion's quay, we attempt a landing at the adjacent supernatural port of the *occult.* It is impossible to tie up here because the docking facility is found to be illusory.

Our mental ship now makes a stopover at the port called *death.* We note here that death does not have a cut and dried definition, and ask: death of what, and when? For example, death of the whole body does not necessarily coincide with the death of its parts. This leads us to probe the definition of death. In so doing, we investigate life suspension, as in a frozen cell, and compare it to what we call death: the irreversible end of life. We note once more that the Saved Memory Hypothesis regards death as an event that fails to permanently interrupt the continuation of memory and consciousness.

Now we drop anchor at a very different and active harbour labelled *life* where we follow the evolution of living things from their first origins to today's organisms. We note that the simplest forms, lacking memories, do not qualify for a post mortem existence according to the Saved Memory Hypothesis. We speculate that the evolution of intelligence, which does not stop at man, may be proceeding at multiple sites in our Universe, and perhaps in parallel domains such as the bubble universes of Andrei Linde and the subatomic world of postulated saved memories.

Our visits to the various ports of call in this book enable us to expand and elaborate upon our hypothesis for the existence of eternal consciousness. It would be surprising if the Reader, my companion during this exploratory voyage, were to believe that any of the concepts of our Hypothesis were valid without prior verification, but he or she could hardly be censured for suspecting that a grain or two of truth might lurk within the recesses of these ideas.

* * * * *

One loose end in this book that can be tied up without further ado concerns the Advocate of saved memories whom we left on a previous page obsessively searching for the author of Surviving Death in order to obtain his autograph.

We come upon the Advocate approaching the local watering hole where the Author is rumoured to be taking liquid refreshment. The Advocate peers through the door to establish which of the drinkers has the appearance of a philosopher. His attention is soon drawn to a gangly, huddled form scribbling on a yellow foolscap pad. Empty bottles adorn his table. The Advocate hoves to, and the following dialogue ensues:

*Advocate* (holding up *Surviving Death):* "Excuse me. Are you by any chance the author of this?"

*Author:* "I am." The voice is languid, but the eyes penetrating.

*Advocate:* "May I have your autograph?" He extends his copy of *Surviving Death,* which the Author duly signs and hands back.

*Author:* "Have a seat."

*Advocate* (hesitating): "I'm not disturbing you?"

*Author* (signaling): "Waiter, bring this man a drink."

*Advocate* (sitting down): "Much obliged." He points to the yellow pad which is covered with scribbled lines. "Writing a new book?"

*Author* (nods and smiles enigmatically): "I am."

*Advocate:* "More on life after death?"

*Author:* "No, this is about complexity." He clears his throat. "About creating order out of chaos."

*Advocate:* "I like your stuff on life after death. I haven't seen that kind of approach before. I was trying to explain it today to some religious chaps."

*Author:* "There's nothing supernatural about my Hypothesis."

*Advocate:* "I know, I know." Hesitates. "But aren't there a few loose ends?"

*Author* (pausing to quaff deeply): "Such as ...?"

*Advocate:* "Well, for example, the Self. If your Self disappears when you're unconscious, why not in death?"

*Author:* "Why not, indeed."

*Advocate:* "I mean, if we're not always conscious during life, why should we be in death?"

*Author:* "Maybe we're not."

*Advocate:* "Then where's your theory?"

*Author:* "It's not a theory, it's a hypothesis."

*Advocate* (less confident): "What about before birth? Where is the Self then?"

*Author* (takes a sip of beer): "If you read my book, you know I'm not a reincarnationist."

*Advocate:* "Well, what about purpose? A plan behind creation. You don't say much about this in your book."

*Author:* "Good point." He taps at his blotchy pad. "I'm taking a look at the subject of purpose in the new book."

*Advocate:* "I've got some ideas on that."

The advocate signals the waiter who brings another round, and both men settle down to a prolonged, if pleasantly wet, discussion of existence.

# BIBLIOGRAPHY OF REFERENCES

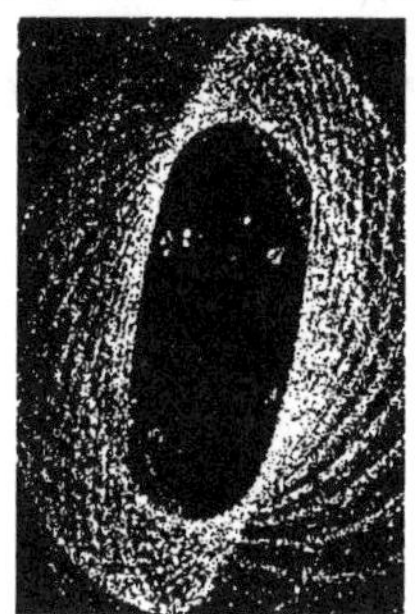


Adams, L. A., and Eddy, S., *Comparative Anatomy,* (John Wiley & Sons, N.Y., 1949)

Adler, M.J., *How to Think about God,* (Collier Books, N.Y., 1991)

Albert, David Z., *Quantum Mechanics and Experience,* (Harvard Univ Press, 1992)

Angus, Samuel, *The Mystery-Religions and Christianity,* (Carol, N.Y., 1966)

Baggott, Jim, *The Meaning of Quantum Theory,* (Oxford Univ Press 1992)

Barnett, Lincoln, *The Universe and Dr. Einstein* (Time Book Division, N.Y., 1962)

Berger, Arthur & Joyce, *Reincarnation,* (Aquarian Press, London, 1991)

Calder, Nigel, *Einstein's Universe,* (Viking Penguin, N.Y., 1979)

Comfort, Alex, *The Biology of Senescence,* (Holt, Rinehart & Winston, N.Y., 1964)

Dennett, Daniel C., *Consciousness Explained,* (Little, Brown & Co., Boston, 1991)

Fawcett, Don, *The Cell,* (W. B. Saunders, N.Y., 1981)

Feynman, Richard, *QED,* (Princeton University Press, New Jersey, 1988)

Finch, C.E., Hayflick, L., *The Biology of Aging,* (Van Nostrand Reinhold, N.Y.1977)

Finkbeiner, Ann K., *At the Point of Singularity,* (Air & Space, Aug/Sept 1993)

Freedman, David H., *Quantum Consciousness,* (Discover, June 1994 )

Ham, A.W., *Histology,* (J.B. Lippincott, Philadelphia, 1965)

Harpur, Tom, *Life After Death,* (McClelland & Stewart, Toronto, 1992)

Hash, J.M., *How Did Life Begin,* (Time Magazine, N.Y., Oct. 11, 1993)

Hawking, Stephen, *A Brief History of Time,* (Bantam Books, N.Y., 1990)

Hawking, Stephen, *Black Holes and Baby Universes,* (Bantam Books, N.Y.,1993)

Hegner, R.W., *College Zoology,* (Macmillan, N.Y., 1947)

Hick, John, *Death and Eternal Life,* (Collins, London, 1976)

Kafatos & Nadeau, *The Conscious Universe,* (Springer-Verlag, 1990)

MacGregor, Geddes, *Images of Afterlife,* (Paragon House, N.Y., 1992)

Madeleine, J., *How Did Life Begin?* (Time, Oct. 1993)

Penrose, Roger, *The Emperor's New Mind,* (Oxford University Press, Oxford, 1989)

Penrose, Roger, *Shadows of the Mind*

Ranson, S.W. & Clark, S.L. *The Anatomy of the Nervous System,* (Saunders, Phila '47)

Rawcliffe, D.H., *Occult & Supernatural Phenomena,* (Dover, N.Y., 1959)

Ross, N.W., *Buddhism* (Vintage Books, N.Y., 1981)

Sagan, Carl, *Cosmos,* (Random House, N.Y., 1983)

Sharp, L.W., *Fundamentals of Cytology,* (McGraw-Hill, N.Y., 1943)

Smith, Huston, *The Religions of Man,* (Harper Perennial, N.Y., 1986)

Strehler, B.L., *Time, Cells, and Aging,* (Academic Press, 1977)

Tipler, Frank J., *The Physics of Immortality*

Watson, J.D., *Molecular Biology of the Gene,* (W.A. Benjamin, N.Y., 1970)

Weinberg, Steven, *Dreams of a Final Theory,* (Pantheon, 1992)

White, Chandler, Smith, *Principles of Biochemistry,* (McGraw-Hill, N.Y., 1959)

Wilson, Colin, *Afterlife,* (Grafton Books, London, 1987)

Wright, Robert, *Science, God, and Man,* (Time Magazine, N.Y., Dec. 28, 1992)

**Scientific American, Inc., 415 Madison Ave., N.Y.**

Angel & Woolf, *Searching for Life on Other Planets,* Apr, 1996

Beardsley, T., *NASA Wants to Fend Off Doomsday Asteroids,* Nov. 1991

Beardsley, Tim, *Dennett's Dangerous Idea,* Feb. 1996

Brush, S.C., *How Cosmology Became a Science,* Aug. 1992

Capecchi, Mario R., *Targeted Gene Replacement,* Mar. 1994

Chalmers, David, *The Puzzle of Conscious Experience,* Dec. 1995

Chiao, R.Y., Kwiat, P.G., Steinberg, A.M., *Faster Than Light?* Aug. '93

Crick, F., & Koch, C., *The Problem of Consciousness,* Sept. 1992

Fischbach, G.D., *Mind and Brain,* Sept. 1992

Freedman, W.L., *The Expansion Rate and Size of the Universe,* Nov. 1992

Gehrels, Tom, *Collisions with Comets and Asteroids,* Mar. 1996

Goldman-Rakik, *Working Memory and the Mind,* Sept. 1992

Gould, Stephen Jay, *The Evolution of Life on the Earth,* Oct. 1994

Hinton, G.E., *How Neural Networks Learn from Experience,* Sept. 1992

Horgan, John, *Measuring Eternity,* Dec. 1990

Horgan, John, *Profile: Edward Witten,* Nov. 1991

Horgan, John, *Profile: Karl R. Popper,* Nov. 1992

Horgan, John, *Quantum Philosophy*, July 1992
Horgan, John, *Can Science Explain Consciousness?* July 1994
Horgan, John, *Particle Metaphysics*, Feb. 1994
Horgan, John, *The Return of the Maverick*, Mar. 1995
Kandel, E.R. & Hawkins, R.D., *The Biological Basis of Learning and Individuality*, Sept. 1992
Kirshner, Robert P., *The Earth's Elements*, Oct. 1994
Levinton, J.S., *The Big Bang of Animal Evolution*, Nov. 1992
Linde, Andrei, *The Self-Reproducing Inflationary Universe*, Nov. 1994
May, R.M., *How Many Species Inhabit the Earth*, Oct. 1992
Miller, P.M., *The Wind and Donald O. Hebb*, Jan. 1993
Minsky, Marvin, *Will Robots Inherit the Earth?* Oct. 1994
Morgan, John, *Off to an Early Start*, Aug. 1993
Morrison, Philip, *Planet-tude*, May 1996
Mukerjee, Madhusree, *Gathering String*, June 1994
Nauen, Stroud, Yeazell, *The Classical Limit of an Atom*, June 1994
Orgel, Leslie E., *The Origin of life on the Earth*, Oct. 1994
Powell, C.S., *The Golden Age of Cosmology*, July 1992
Powe1l, C.S., *Star Gobbler*, Aug. 1994
Powell, Corey, *Strange Places*, Jan. 1996
Raichle, Marcus E., *Visualizing the Mind*, April 1994
Rebek, Julius, Jr., *Synthetic Self-Replicating Molecules*, July 1994
Rees, M.J., *Black Holes in Galactic Centers*, Nov. 1990
Sagan, Carl, *The Search for Extraterrestrial Life*, Oct. 1994
Schramm, Peebles, & Kron, Turner, *The Evolution of the Universe*, Oct '94
Selkoe, D.J., *Aging Brain, Aging Mind*, Sept. 1992
Skatz, C.J., *The Developing Brain*, Sept. 1992
Storey, K.B. & J.M., *Frozen and Alive*, Dec. 1990
Van Den Bergh, S., & Hessnet, J.E., *How the Milky Way Formed*, Jan. '93
Webster & White, *The Genetic Basis of Cancer*, Mar. 1995
Weinberg, Steven, *Life in the Universe*, Oct. 1994
York, Derek, *The Earliest History of the Earth*, Jan. 1993

**The World Book Encyclopedia, Chicago, 1983**
Adams, C.J., *Islam*, vol.10
Adams, C.J., *Muslims*, vol.13
Brown, J.H., *Evolution*, vol.6
Capps, W.H., *Religion*, vol.16
Ellison, S.P.,Jr., *Earth*, vol.6
Falk, N.E.Auer, *Mysticism*, vol.13
Hartl, D.L., & Johan, G., *Mendel*, vol.13
Hartl, D.L., *Heredity*, vol.9
Hartl, D.L., *Mutation*, vol.13
Jick, L.A., *Jews*, vol.11
Johnson, R.F., *Bible*, vol.2
Littleton, C.S., *Mythology*, vol.13
Neusner, Jacob, *Judaism*, vol.11
Pond, C.M., *Darwin, Charles Robert*, vol.5
Reynolds, F.E., *Buddhism*, vol.2
Rigby, P.W.J., *Genetics*, vol.8
Rubenstein, Irwin, *Cell*, vol.3
White, C.S.J., *Hinduism*, vol.9

# INDEX